Problem Regions of Europe
General Editor: **D. I. Scargill**

Randstad Holland
G. R. P. Lawrence

OXFORD UNIVERSITY PRESS

Oxford University Press, Ely House, London W.1
Glasgow New York Toronto Melbourne Wellington
Cape Town Ibadan Nairobi Dar es Salaam Lusaka Addis Ababa
Delhi Bombay Calcutta Madras Karachi Lahore Dacca
Kuala Lumpur Singapore Hong Kong Tokyo

© Oxford University Press 1973

First published 1973
Reprinted 1974

All rights reserved. No part of this publication may be reproduced, stored in a retrieval system, or transmitted, in any form or by any means, electronic, mechanical, photocopying, recording or otherwise, without the prior permission of Oxford University Press

Notes on terminology

Holland: Although the title of this book is Randstad Holland, the word 'Holland' is only used elsewhere when referring to the two provinces of North Holland and South Holland in the west of the country. The name for the whole country is the Netherlands (Nederland) and the adjective for the people is Dutch

Dike: This spelling is used throughout the book (as opposed to the alternative 'dyke'). The feature in question is a defensive wall used to keep water away from other land, i.e. to prevent sea-water from flooding low-lying areas or to keep river and canal waters to their course. Additional dikes may be built as second and third lines of defence behind the main 'walls'.

Filmset by BAS Printers Limited, Wallop, Hampshire
and printed in Great Britain
at the University Press, Oxford
by Vivian Ridler, Printer to the University

Editor's Preface

Great economic and social changes have taken place in Europe in recent years. The agricultural labour force has almost everywhere contracted, in some places very rapidly, and the lack of alternative forms of employment in rural areas has resulted in large-scale movements of farmers and farm labourers in search of work in the cities. The scale of this drift from the land can be gauged from the fact that in the six (original) Common Market countries the agricultural work force was halved between 1950 and 1970: from approximately 20 millions to 10 millions. In many areas this rural exodus has made it possible to carry out much needed reorganization of farm holdings, but it has also brought with it problems concerning, for example, the provision of services to a contracting population and the need to establish new forms of land use where farming is no longer profitable.

Contraction of the labour force has also taken place in several old-established industries. These include coal-mining, shipbuilding, and the more traditional textile industries, where the effects of a shrinking market have been made more severe by automation, which has substituted machines for men. The coal-mining industry of Western Europe shed something like two-thirds of its labour force during the 1950s and 1960s. Wherever a large proportion of the working population was dependent upon a declining industry of this kind, the problems of adjustment have been severe. Many schemes have been devised to attract alternative forms of employment but, despite incentives, it has often proved difficult to attract new firms because of the old industrial areas' legacy of dirt, derelict landscape, poor housing, and, in some places, bad labour relations.

Problems of a different kind have arisen as a result of the continued growth of large cities such as London and Paris, or of groups of closely related cities as in the case of Randstad Holland. The reasons for such growth are several. To the manufacturer the big city offers the advantage of a local market, a varied labour force, and easy access to suppliers and other manufacturers with whom he needs to maintain close links. To them and even more to the service industries a city location offers a prestige location, and the enormous expansion of service activity, especially office-work, has contributed greatly to postwar urban growth. Attempts to control the increase of employment within cities have had some success as far as manufacturing industry is concerned but very little with regard to office work.

Problems resulting from city growth include traffic congestion, high land prices, pollution, and social stress brought about by factors such as housing shortages and travelling long distances to work. Yet the city continues to attract migrants for whom the image is still one of streets paved with gold, whilst the established resident is loath to leave the 'bright lights', the football club, or the familiar shops.

Geographers, in the past, have been reluctant to focus their attention on regional problems. The problem was thought to be a temporary phenomenon and therefore less worthy of consideration than regional characteristics of a more enduring nature—the landscape or the chimerical *personality* of the region. Yet such is the magnitude, persistence, and areal extent of problems of the kind referred to above that the geographer would seem to be well justified in approaching his regional study by seeking to identify, measure, and even seek solutions to problems.

'Devenant alors un cadre de recherche, la région sera choisie en fonction de certains problèmes et des moyens qui permettent de les aborder avec profit' (H. Baulig). Indeed it has been suggested that regions can be defined in terms of the problems with which they are confronted.

Additional stimulus for studying regional problems arises from the interest which politicians and planners have recently shown in the region as a framework for tackling such issues as the relief of unemployment, the siting of new investment, and the reorganization of administrative boundaries. Governments have long been aware of the problems resulting from economic and social changes and various attempts have been made to solve them. Development Areas and New Towns in Great Britain, for example, represent an attempt to deal with the problems, on the one hand, of the declining industrial areas and, on the other, of the overgrown cities. Such solutions can hardly be described as regional, however. Other countries have recognized the problems of their overpopulated rural areas and the Cassa per il

Mezzogiorno, the Fund for the South, was set up by the Italian government in 1950 in order to encourage investment in the South. The E.E.C. has also channelled funds via its Investment Bank, both to southern Italy and to other parts of the Common Market distant from the main centres of economic activity. Planning of this kind shows an awareness of the regional extent of economic and social problems, though in practice much of the actual work of planning was undertaken on a piecemeal, local, and short-term basis.

Since about 1960, however, the continuing nature of the problems has persuaded most European governments to adopt longer-term and more comprehensive planning measures, and the importance of seeking regional solutions has been increasingly stressed. The last ten years have, in fact, witnessed the setting up of regional planning authorities in many European countries and to them has been given the task of identifying regional problems and of finding solutions to them. A large number of reports have been published following research carried out by these authorities, and individual governments have introduced regional considerations to national planning. The French *métropoles d'équilibre*, for example, were devised in order to introduce new vigour to the regions via the largest provincial towns.

One of the drawbacks to regional planning of this kind is the outdated nature of local government boundaries, most planning decisions having to be implemented through a system of local government more suited to nineteenth than to late twentieth century conditions. Some experts have thus advocated a regional alternative to existing local government areas, and it is interesting to note that the Royal Commission on Local Government in England (the Maud Report), whilst not supporting so radical a change, nevertheless introduced the idea of *provinces* within which broad planning policies could be carried out. Supporters of the regional idea argue that a growing trend toward State centralization is bringing about a reaction in the form of renewed popular interest in regions, their history, industrial archaeology, customs, dialect, and so on.

The revival of interest in regions, both for their own sake and as a practical aid to planning or administration, makes particularly timely the appearance of a series of geographical studies concerned with *Problem Regions of Europe*. The present volume is one of 12 studies comprising such a series.

The twelve regions have been selected in order to illustrate, between them, a variety of problems. The most obvious of these are: problems of a harsh environment, of isolation, of industrial decay, of urban congestion, and of proximity to a sensitive political frontier. One or other of these major problems forms the dominant theme in each of the volumes of the series, but they have not been studied in isolation. Where it has been thought relevant to do so, authors have drawn attention to similar problems encountered in other parts of the continent so that readers may compare both the causes of problems and the methods employed to solve them. At the same time it is recognized that every region has a number of problems that are unique to itself and these peculiarly local problems have been distinguished from those of a more general kind.

Although the precise treatment of each subject will vary according to the nature of the region concerned and, to some extent, the outlook of a particular author, readers will find much in common in the arrangement of contents in each volume. In each of them the nature of the problem or problems which characterize the region is first stated by the author; next the circumstances that have given rise to the problems are explained; after this the methods that have been employed to overcome the problems are subjected to critical examination and evaluation. Each study includes indications of likely future developments.

All the authors of the series have considerable first-hand knowledge of the regions about which they have written. Yet none of them would claim to have a complete set of answers to any particular regional problem. For this reason, as well as from a desire to make the series challenging, each volume contains suggestions for further lines of inquiry that the reader may pursue. The series was conceived initially as one that would be helpful to sixth-form geographers but it is believed that individual volumes will also provide a useful introduction to the detailed work undertaken by more advanced students both of geography and of European studies in general.

D.I.S.

St. Edmund Hall
August 1972

Contents

		page
1	**Introduction**	7
2	**Main Characteristics**	8
3	**Regions of the Randstad**	10
4	**Agriculture**	18
	Horticulture and market gardening	18
	Arable farming	20
	Cattle and other livestock	21
	Size of agricultural holdings	21
5	**Industries**	22
	Iron and steel	22
	Oil and chemicals	23
	Other industries	24
6	**Population**	25
	Distribution and density	25
	Population characteristics	26
7	**Towns and Urbanization**	28
	Town growth	28
	Urbanization	29
	Population change	29
	Hierarchical relationships	30
8	**Transport and Communications**	32
	Water links	32
	Roads	35
	Railways	35
	Air traffic	37
	Pipelines and powerlines	37
9	**Planning the Solution**	39
	General considerations	39
	The Randstad	40
	Administrative organization	42
	Major projects	43
10	**Conclusion**	44
	Further Work	46
	Appendix	47
	Index	48

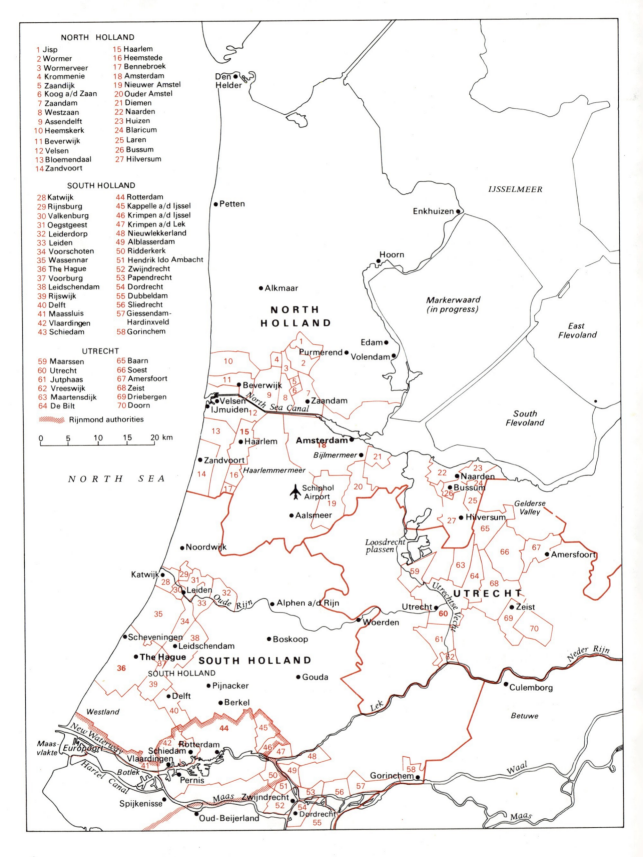

1 Introduction

The Randstad region of the Netherlands is unlike many of the problem regions of Europe in that it is the metropolitan centre of a thriving and prosperous nation. Even so, prosperity brings problems, and hence there are conflicts of land-use requirements in which national, local, and personal needs may well seem to be at cross-purposes.

The physical limits of the region are clear and well known. The North Sea to the west, the IJsselmeer to the east and the Rhine/Maas distributaries to the south form well-defined boundaries. Within this area there are a number of historic cities, which planners and geographers have come to know collectively as Randstad Holland. Use of this term is not to underestimate the importance of each individual city but to underline the common considerations facing them all, considerations resulting from their position in geographical space, their historical evolution, the social factors of increasing population and changing demands for the wherewithal of modern life—housing, communications, recreation, and an acceptable environment.

Unlike other European problem areas, where major difficulties have been created by the industrial expansion of the nineteenth century, the industries of the Netherlands are relatively modern. Nevertheless, Dutch city centres are in need of urban renewal and re-structuring, to reduce overcrowding and to remove traffic congestion. Special problems in this area are obviously created by the environment, in which flat delta land at or below sea-level has necessitated drainage, and there has been a tendency to crowd buildings into the historic core areas.

In order to appreciate these problems it is first necessary to establish the geographical characteristics of the area as a whole and of its regional subdivisions. Secondly, it is important that the geographical themes which underlie the problems are isolated and understood. Finally, some of the proposals for their solution must be examined. Inevitably some interweaving of these three strands must occur and allowance must always be made for the changes brought about by continuing development.

Fig. 1 (*opposite*). The Randstad urban municipalities and other places mentioned in the text. Population figures for the seventy numbered municipalities are listed in the Appendix

2 Main Characteristics

The western and most urbanized section of the Netherlands is formed by the provinces of North Holland, South Holland, and Utrecht; and more specifically by the urban regions around Amsterdam, The Hague, Rotterdam, and Utrecht, forming a nearly complete ring of towns.

That this is the most populated area in the Netherlands is clear from the most recent population census (see Appendix) and can be summarized as follows (1.1.71):

Population of the Netherlands   13 119 430
Population of province of
    North Holland: 2 259 955
    South Holland: 2 991 735   } 6 068 059
    Utrecht: 816 369

Although this last figure represents 46·2 per cent of the population, yet the total area of these three provinces (759 312 hectares) is only about 21 per cent of that of the Netherlands as a whole.

This high concentration of population is confined to an area of distinctive and challenging land, namely the delta lands of the rivers Rhine and Maas. The natural resources of the region can only be described as somewhat meagre, although its intensive agricultural and horticultural activities are justly renowned. Power resources are represented by an oilfield, producing just a fraction of the Dutch national requirements (Table 2, p. 22).

Possibly the major resource of the Randstad area is its position: the North Sea and the Rhine are major trade axes and the great industrial hinterland in West Germany requires well developed access to the world trade routes via the North Sea. Additionally, the population of these provinces of the Netherlands inherits a tradition of marketing, trade, and commercial enterprise. Together with skills acquired by centuries of intensive farming, fishing, engineering, urban development, and civilization generally, the Dutch are able to use the position of their country to good advantage in the modern European scene.

The name Randstad has been used specifically for a number of years to denote the group of towns in the western Netherlands located adjacent to the polders of Holland. Literally, the word translates as 'rim city', as of settlements on the edge of a saucer. The expression 'greenheart city' has also been used (Burke, 1966) for this phenomenon and draws attention to the basically open and rural central area of Randstad. The term 'conurbation'—implying a group of towns which, although linked, still maintain their own individuality—can well be applied to this area whilst the expression 'urban zone' conveys something of the essential features of the region and has been used by the Dutch Government Second Report on Physical Planning in the Netherlands (1966).

Contained almost entirely within the three Dutch provinces of South Holland, North Holland and Utrecht, the Randstad is unique in that the whole conurbation forms metropolitan Netherlands, yet the functions normally found in one city are distributed between the main centres. Thus, the centre of government is The Hague (in Dutch *Den Haag*, but also called *s'Gravenhage*), the formal capital of the country is Amsterdam, the main port facilities lie in and west of Rotterdam, and so on.

Despite the apparently large extent of ground covered by the Randstad (1712 square kilometres for the principal agglomerations, excluding the open interior which would more than double this figure) it can be noted that the total area of the western Holland region is about comparable with the size of Greater Los Angeles or Greater London with its Green Belt (e.g. Slough to Dartford and Luton to Redhill). Whereas these and other world cities such as Paris are examples of the outward spread of a single major centre, swallowing others in a nearly continuous mass of urban amenities, Randstad consists of towns and cities built around open countryside in which rural activities and agriculture remain important.

The problem nature of the Randstad can best be considered as a mixture of general problems posed by its situation and development together with particular problems of individual areas which must be looked at separately. Each urban centre has its own character and personality, stemming from factors of site and historical development, although a number of common elements can be recognized. The importance of drainage and the construction of dikes has resulted in particular town layouts exemplified by the Dike Towns or Dike-and-Dam Towns recognized

The Hague Municipality

The recently developed suburban extension of the Hague at Mariahoeve. The view shows the rural edge of this development with a series of horticultural glasshouse plots

by Burke. Where harbours were also constructed a further variation is found, but the canal in a loop or even forming a complete circle around the town is a commonplace feature of both small and large towns. In the largest, such as Amsterdam, a series of canals mark concentric growth rings. Today, some of these urban features may be serious obstacles to central redevelopment and the ring dike may be a potential line for a new road. A compromise solution seems to have been reached in Utrecht where *part* of the central dike is to be used for new roadworks. Local or municipal plans must deal with individual conflicts of land-use and physical planning and must take account of transport, industrialization, and the environment. The Randstad forms an entity within the Netherlands, but it is an entity consisting of individual cells. The development of this one region is of consequence for the whole country and must accord with national needs.

3 Regions of the Randstad

It is possible to sub-divide the Randstad in a variety of different ways but in this section a series of functional regions, twenty-one in number, have been used for the purposes of brief regional description. These regions show considerable variety of scale and of importance (when considered nationally or locally) and range from the rural central area in which dairying and agricultural products are important, to the heavy industrial complex of the IJ mouth (IJmond area of IJmuiden-Velsen).

Residential service functions are characteristic of several of these regional sub-divisions of the Randstad and they provide for a commuting population which works in the nearby city or industrial area. Thus, Amsterdam is served by South Kennemerland and Het Gooi, Rotterdam and The Hague by the Wassenaar area, and Utrecht by the Heuvelrug district of the glacial ridge country to the east. Part of this latter region also serves as a residential area for Amsterdam, and there are considerable cross-movements from all of these residential areas to work elsewhere in the Randstad, not necessarily to the nearest centre or region. Similarly, the entire Randstad has links beyond its immediate borders and the definition of the area as a whole poses some problems for the geographer and planner. For the purposes of description four differing regional groupings can be considered:

A. The western Netherlands group of provinces—North Holland, South Holland, and Utrecht—which includes peninsular Holland.
B. The seventy 'urbanized' municipalities shown on Fig. 1 (page 6).
C. The generalized horseshoe-shaped area referred to as the Randstad in various published accounts (e.g. Peter Hall, *The World Cities*).
D. The functional regions, based on economic and geographical considerations, used in the following pages and shown on Fig. 2.

1 Amsterdam agglomeration

This region is centred on the capital and includes a great variety of urban land-use. As a port, Amsterdam is dominated by importing activities for the entire Netherlands with associated food and manufacturing industries. It is a national distribution centre for many commodities and also a centre for services such as banking and insurance. Amsterdam is the capital of the Netherlands and is the city with the largest population (820 406 at 1 January 1971). The agglomeration is dominated by the city and is highly metropolitan in character, with the notable exception of central government activities, which are located at The Hague (below). Amsterdam has an urban core of great distinction, having its original site at the point of confluence of the tributary river Amstel with the Rhine distributary, the IJ. A dam was constructed across the Amstel in 1240 and this river was then diverted around the nucleus of the town. Successive later diversions created a series of approximately concentric semi-circles of canals which give the city centre its characteristic form. Present-day functions which dominate this core area are those of banking, finance, and the commercial activities of a major shopping centre. Luxury trades, ranging from the diamond industry to clothing, the printing industry, art galleries, museums, hotels, and shops catering for the

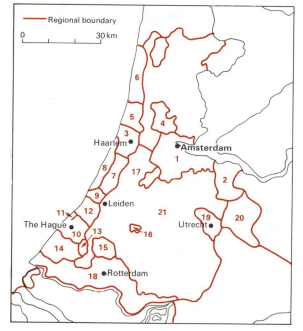

Fig. 2. Functional regions of the Randstad

tourist trade are all represented in close proximity within this section of the city.

Processing industries, chiefly of foodstuffs such as cacao and sugar, breweries and the distilling of spirits, timber-yards, and storage depots for oil products are present in the outer industrial zone. This is located chiefly to the north-west of the city at the entrance to the North Sea Canal (built in the 1870s). North of the IJ is the heavy industrial area, including dry docks, whilst new industrial areas are planned for the south-east as well as in the main growth area along the North Sea Canal, which is where the Mobil oil refinery is sited at the end of the pipeline from Europoort. The international airport at Schiphol, immediately south-west of the municipal boundary of Amsterdam, has associated industrial development, e.g. the Fokker aircraft works.

The development of Amsterdam's suburbs has resulted in the city swallowing older villages and also in several extensions of the municipal boundaries over the years. This growth has been generally southwards and those areas which are outside the original muncipality but which clearly form part of the agglomeration include Amstelveen, Sloetermeer, and Osdorp. Recent housing developments are at Bijlmermeer where a suburban new town area is approaching completion.

2 Het Gooi
3 South Kennemerland

Lying respectively east and west of Amsterdam itself, but forming part of the northern Randstad agglomeration, these two areas provide service functions for a chiefly residential population. They are the main commuter zones for Amsterdam, but travel to work is not confined to this one city. The Het Gooi area is on the gradually more undulating land of the low hills formed on Pleistocene glacial materials (this in fact marks the westernmost position of the Riss ice sheet in the Netherlands). Land heights do not rise more than 20 metres above sea-level but this affords a considerable contrast with the below-sea-level altitudes common elsewhere in the Randstad. The main centres of population are Hilversum and Bussum, and both these towns have industrial activities—carpets, chemicals, and light metal industries—as well as telecommunications being represented. Naarden, a former port on the Zuider Zee, is contiguous with Bussum and both these towns perform tourist and holiday-centre roles.

The South Kennemerland area west of Amsterdam is centred on Haarlem. Although this is an important residential and commuting area for Amsterdam and other Randstad cities, it too has industries, particularly in metal engineering,

The characteristic layout of central Amsterdam, with parallel, almost concentric, semicircular canals is clearly seen in this air view. The approximate limit of the eighteenth century is marked by the change of housing pattern near the bottom left of the picture. The nineteenth-century extension incorporating the Central railway station is at the top, with part of the harbour beyond

Aerofilms

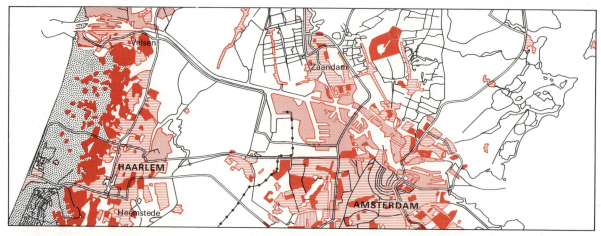

Fig. 3. Ijmuiden—Amsterdam area

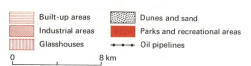

Key to Figs. 3 and 4

cacao, and printing. The suburbs of Haarlem extend on to the dune coastal strip, but the chief tourist areas here are considered as part of functional region 7 (below) although Haarlem and Zaandvoort (on the coast) very nearly meet.

4 The Zaan

An industrial region north of Amsterdam is centred on the town of Zaandam and includes other settlements associated with the Zaan, a principal dike and former right bank distributary of the IJ, blocked at both ends since the reclamation of this area in the thirteenth century. This was once a major shipbuilding region but the industry has declined, the present-day major concentration of shipbuilding being at Rotterdam with some work at Amsterdam. The region's earlier links with overseas Dutch possessions resulted in the establishment of some of the foodstuffs industries here, but in addition to this are wood-working industries, and food industries based on local vegetable, dairy, and meat products. As well as local industries the Zaan area provides some commuter traffic to Amsterdam, with good communications via the Coen road tunnel beneath the North Sea Canal.

5 IJ mouth (IJmond)

This is the heavy industrial region of North Holland and it is located, together with a fishing port complex, at the seaward end of the North Sea Canal. The opening of this canal in 1876 was designed to provide a good sea link for Amsterdam and to effect the reclamation of polders marking the former course of the IJ. At the North Sea end various locks have superseded the original inadequate ones and the present locks are amongst the world's largest. A state-constructed fishing port with harbour and associated settlements is located on the southern side of the North Sea entrance to the canal and the Hoogovens complex of the iron and steel industry, power station, etc. is at Velsen, immediately inland (page 22).

6 North Kennemerland
7 South Kennemerland and Rijnland coastal areas

These districts include sections of the coastal dune belt and, in the north, the polders behind them. Recreational functions, tourism, camping grounds, and hotels predominate here with the main centres at Katwijk, Noordwijk, and Zaandvoort. These dunes are also important for water supply, natural ground water being supplemented by artificial filtration of water piped from the Rhine.

8 Bollenstreek
9 Rijnsburg

Horticulture, especially bulb cultivation in the Bollenstreek area and market gardening of flowers and vegetables, characterize these two areas. The particular dominance of bulb preparation has led to the formation of a distinctive landscape of smallholdings in rectangular hedged plots (for shelter) with many access canals and a very carefully controlled water table level. Dairy

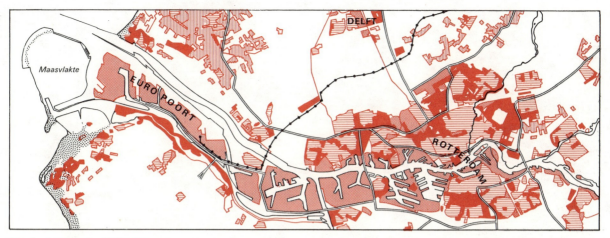

Fig. 4. Europoort—Rotterdam

farming, especially with pig rearing included, is also found.

The Rijnsburg area at the mouth of the Old Rhine, west of Leiden, is chiefly concerned with the cultivation of vegetables, many of which are canned or frozen at Leiden. This town is the regional centre for the mid-western Randstad and also has engineering and metal industries.

10 The Hague agglomeration
11 Scheveningen
12 Wassenaar
13 Delft

The western end of the southern belt of settlement in the Randstad is centred on The Hague. This city was previously the capital of The Netherlands and is today the seat of government as well as housing the majority of official and administrative institutions. Delft is an old established manufacturing town and possesses pottery works (the famous blue porcelain ware) and distilleries. Considerable residential development is taking place in the region north-east of Delft towards Zoetermeer. Wassenaar and Scheveningen are mainly residential areas with a commuting population chiefly employed in The Hague and Rotterdam, although Scheveningen is also an important coastal tourist centre with its nucleus around an original fishing village.

14 Westland
15 Berkel
16 Boskoop
17 Aalsmeer

These four areas are grouped together as they are all regions of horticultural or market gardening specialities. The Westland and Berkel market gardening areas are nearly adjacent concentrations within the agricultural south-west portion of the Randstad, whilst Boskoop and Aalsmeer are separate localities. Nevertheless, all four sub-regions show marked specialization in the intensive agricultural sector. Westland and Berkel are particularly important for vegetable cultivation under glass (especially tomatoes) whilst the Aalsmeer area has more of a specialism in flowers (also under glass). Boskoop is particularly noted for roses and shrubs.

18 Rotterdam agglomeration

Along both banks of the New Waterway (Nieuwe Waterweg) and upstream along the Rhine distributaries of the Maas and Waal to Dordrecht and Gorinchem there is a continuous zone of industrial and residential development (Fig. 4). At its western end this begins with the packet station of the Hook of Holland (car and lorry ferry to Harwich) on the north bank and the new quays and reclaimed area of Europoort on the south bank. This will be extended further west into the North Sea with the eventual completion of the Maasvlakte reclamation.

Much of this development has taken place during the last twenty years and has been partly the result of changes in methods of international transport: the development of container traffic and bulk movements of raw materials. This area is also Western Europe's major oil port with five refineries, extensive petrochemical industries, and pipeline terminals. These latter take oil to Amsterdam, the Ruhr, and the southern Netherlands. Shipbuilding and many manufacturing industries are also represented here, the latter ranging from chocolate production and breweries to margarine, glassware, and clothing.

The central area of Utrecht is demarcated by a winding canal system, part of which can be seen on the left of this picture. The administrative area of the city and the old university core are partly sited round the cathedral (the nave of which was destroyed by storm in 1674)

19 Utrecht agglomeration

Whereas both Amsterdam and Rotterdam have the special characteristics associated with seaports, and also the problems of cities built on land below sea-level, Utrecht has the more conventional role of a communications centre and provincial capital, sited at the point where land liable to flood rises above the datum level.

Utrecht is an old established ecclesiastical centre, university town, and principal focus of rail routes (the headquarters of the Dutch railway system is here), as well as having a number of industries in printing and food manufacture, and a steelworks. Suburban expansion is onto the higher ground of the glacial ridge especially to the north-east, where a completely new housing area is proposed. Development to the south extends as far as the motorway whilst that to the east includes a new university site with multi-storey buildings.

20 The Utrecht glacial ridge

East of Utrecht, a number of mainly residential areas are interspersed with the wooded heathlands of the glacial ridge, which rises in altitude to a little over 100 metres. To the east again is the Gelderse Valley, which is outside the limits of the Randstad region, but on the boundary between ridge and valley is the town of Amersfoort. Here are mixed metal, chemical, and light industries and the town has good communications with Utrecht, Hilversum, and Amsterdam.

In various parts of the interior of the Randstad flooded sections of countryside represent regions once worked for peat or other materials. Today these can form useful amenities for fishing, water-sports, and as recreation areas generally. The numerous moored boats in the foreground indicate the intensity of use

This area is notably less well endowed for agriculture than region 21 but it does provide a useful area of open land that can be regarded as an amenity for the eastern Randstad, with scenic heathlands and park areas.

21 The Central Region of the Randstad

The greenheart of the Randstad is a predominantly rural region in which the agricultural scene is most evident. Nevertheless, there are locally various special urban and industrial functions and within the region there are also concentrations on particular forms of agricultural production, as well as distinctive landscapes. Since all this area lies at or below sea level it is organized into various water-control zones, and many polders mark stages in the reclamation of the area (Fig. 5). The soils of the central area include considerable areas of peat-based materials and also clays. Certain of the reclaimed areas, from which peat has been removed, are on old marine clays which date from the late Pleistocene period but most of the clays in the south-western section are considerably younger, dating from sub-Boreal and sub-Atlantic times. At about the same time, considerable quantities of silt were being brought into the area by the main rivers so that those districts adjacent to the Rhine/Maas distributaries such as the Waal, Lek, Oude Rijn, and Utrechtse Vecht, are marked by deposits of riverine clays.

The historical development of this area was

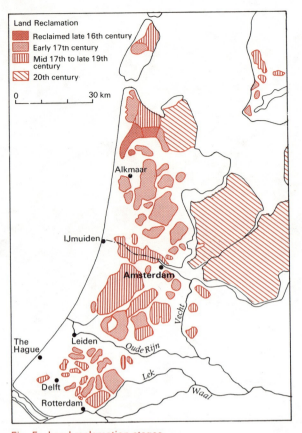

Fig. 5. Land reclamation stages

one of piecemeal reclamation (Fig. 5) so that road lines and field patterns are related to the shape of former lakes and later schemes of polder construction. The largest and one of the most recent of these was the Harlemmermeer polder, completed in 1852 and previously used as a drainage *boezem** for Amsterdam. The soils here are based on Old Sea Clays and are today extensively used for arable cultivation. Regular rectangular fields and farms mark this area although, in fact, this was not formally set out into 20 hectare blocks (and farms of up to 100 hectares extent) until the 1880s.

The former working of peat in parts of this region has resulted in the formation of lagoons somewhat reminiscent of the Norfolk Broads of East Anglia. However, because of very rectilinear land boundaries (which often remain, despite the flooded areas around them) there is a distinctive appearance to this area which is now much used for recreational purposes—for swimming, fishing, boating, etc. and, when frozen in winter, also for ice sports. The Loosdrecht *plassen*† are typical of this facet of the landscape of the central Randstad.

Throughout the Randstad area water drainage is a perpetual necessity and this is accomplished today by a variety of oil- and electrically-driven pumps. The stages of pumping are into successively higher ditches and dikes before finally entering the sea and this will result in a series of pumps, probably arranged as a 'staircase' or 'gang'. Originally the power for such pumping machinery came from the wind, and a large number of windmills remain today as a picturesque part of the landscape in the central Randstad and elsewhere.

**boezem*: the term used to describe a body of water or polder contained within a drainage system.

†*plassen*: a term used to describe inland bodies of water, often abandoned mineral or peat workings, used for recreational purposes such as sailing.

Geographical themes

The preceding pages have provided a general description of the main regional characteristics of these western provinces of the Netherlands which comprise Randstad Holland. Much additional material can be gleaned from other printed sources and the published topographic maps (see Further Work, p. 46).

Certain main themes are seen to occur frequently when one examines the Randstad and these now merit study in a somewhat more systematic manner. These themes correspond with the basic elements of the region's geography which have shaped the present landscape and which, by their interaction, produce those problems which this book is about. They may be listed as follows:

1. Agriculture. Basically the Netherlands is an agricultural country and within the densely-peopled landscape of the Randstad are some of the most intensively farmed areas of Western Europe.
2. Industries. Although not an area of long-established traditional industries, the Randstad includes a substantial part of the industrial employment of the Netherlands.
3. Population. Most of the problems of the Randstad can be related to population pressures resulting in features such as the expansion of towns, the need for communications, and conflicts of land utilization.
4. Towns and urbanization. Although linked with population growth it is necessary to consider some of the features of town growth in the Randstad as a separate topic. This is also true of:
5. Transport and communications.

Each of these subjects will now be considered in turn.

This photograph shows the northern outskirts of Amsterdam with recent 'high-rise' dwellings in the centre, compared with ribbon housing development along the road to Oostzaan in the background. Other modern development at lower levels and slightly older in style can be seen in the foreground. The rural field pattern at the top of the picture is characteristic of this section of the outer Amsterdam area, the Waterland area.

Amsterdam Municipality

4 Agriculture

The low-lying fields and polders of the western Netherlands, below sea-level and in constant need of drainage, conjure up a mental picture of intensive dairying and horticultural activities. There are definite districts in which these are predominant but arable farms and farms with mixed livestock are also to be found. Farm sizes vary considerably, and although they can be composed of small fields in the intensive horticultural areas, there are parts with quite large fields in many districts of arable and grassland cultivation.

Some of the specialized farming regions have been described as functional regions of the Randstad on pages 12–16 and Fig. 2. A general map of farming types in the western Netherlands forms Fig. 6, and Figs. 2 and 6 can therefore be regarded as complementary. It is useful to look at these agricultural characteristics in more detail.

Horticulture and market gardening

The most distinctive agricultural activity in the western Netherlands is that of intensive horticulture. This takes a number of forms. In the Westland area, for example, is a major concentration of vegetable production both in glasshouses and in the open. Some 1400 hectares of glasshouses for tomatoes, lettuces, and cucumber production make this area appear built-up and industrialized. Other crops include cauliflowers, carrots, spinach, leeks, and Brussels sprouts. Open-field cultivation of these crops totals an additional 2500 hectares.

A further region of vegetable-growing in the southern Randstad is known as the 'Kring' district and this lies north and west of Rotterdam, including Berkel, Pijnacker, and Leidschendam (towards Delft and The Hague). Whereas there are a number of different types of vegetables produced in the Westland area, the Kring region concentrates on the salad crops of lettuce, cucumber, and tomatoes. Other more dispersed areas, concentrating on vegetables (and including areas of glasshouses) lie on the southern side of the New Waterway and in the islands of South Holland, for example, the municipality of Zwijndrecht. With improved accessibility, more of this southern zone could well be opened up for intensive horticulture and market gardening.

Although flowers and vegetables are of principal significance in terms both of areas under cultivation and of value, fruit production (soft fruit and fruit under glass, ranging from melons to dessert grapes) also occurs in the western Netherlands. Orchard production is particularly found in the Gelderland area—between the rivers Rhine, Waal, and Maas—and in the Utrecht district.

Flower cultivation and the production of bulbs are further traditional forms of horticultural activity in the Randstad. Bulb-farming requires chalky or sandy soils but certain clays are also favoured. The main region, the Bollenstreek, lies between Haarlem and Leiden and this small area accounts for about half the Dutch total area of bulb production. The bulbs concerned are tulips, daffodils, narcissi, gladioli and hyacinths. A considerable area (more than 10 000 hectares) is devoted to this form of cultivation in North and South Holland but as this is divided amongst more than 8000 holdings in these two provinces the actual size of each holding is quite small. The value of the Dutch total bulbs output in 1970 was 284 million guilders (£34 million) so this represents an important source of revenue to the Netherlands (Table 1).

Flower cultivation is partly under glass (the Netherlands total is 1642 hectares) and partly in the open (917 hectares), with the Aalsmeer region being of major importance. In this area the industry is highly organized and by means of road, rail, and air (Schiphol airport) quick marketing is possible. Local specialisms are in roses and house plants at Aalsmeer and Berkel-Rodenrijs (near Rotterdam). The cultivation of shrubs, conifers, and rhododendrons is highly concentrated in the Boskoop area. This is a particularly interesting form of concentration as it is helped by the establishment of a carefully regulated water table in the surrounding polders.

The Dutch concern with the development of intensive agricultural activities can be attributed to a number of considerations. First, relatively favourable soil and climatic factors are coupled with a good water supply. Secondly, despite the earlier lack of industry in the Netherlands, a tradition of marketing and merchant enterprise has resulted in an urban society requiring large quantities of food. The production of high value foodstuffs, grown on relatively limited land areas to supply a local as well as a developing market in

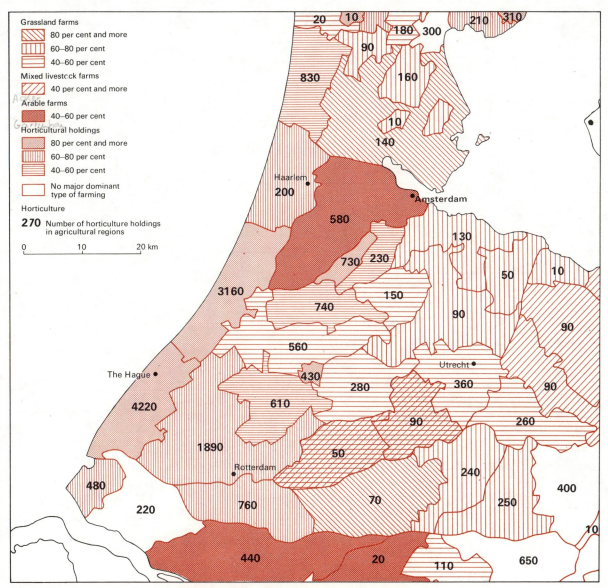

Fig. 6. Farming types in the western Netherlands

TABLE I
Horticultural production in the Netherlands

	Value (in million guilders)		Area under glass (in hectares)		Area in the open (in hectares)	
	1958	1970	1958	1970	1958	1970
Vegetables	374	1 103	3 561	5 379	33 507	45 503
Fruit	177	216	471	212	53 925	38 280
Bulbs	148	284	—	—	8 236	12 365
Flowers and plants	111	555	459	1 642	978	917
Trees	37	110	9	20	2 795	3 803
Seeds	16	23	—	—	—	—
Total	887	2 334	4 500	7 253	99 441	100 868

Gross Output (value at constant prices) 1958=100, 1970=189
Labour Force (in horticulture) 1963=100, 1970=70

Boskoop. The horticultural specialism of this region is the cultivation of shrubs, generally in the open, although one glasshouse is visible in this view. The canal is a relatively minor one linking the Oude Rijn (at Alphen) and the Hollandsche Ijssel (at Gouda). Nevertheless it carries quite substantial barge traffic, and its crossing bridges are all of the lifting variety shown here. Roads follow the line of the dikes, and the settlement of Boskoop is a good example of a 'dike village'. Recent road improvements on the road to Alphen (top right) have caused a line to be taken across the polders

nearby industrial countries (Great Britain, Germany, Belgium) thus characterized the later nineteenth-century development of Dutch agriculture. Thirdly, relatively cheap supplies of fodder grains from overseas stimulated the concentration on livestock products, particularly those derived from dairy cattle. Horticultural specialization can be ascribed to the position of the Netherlands in relation to an immense market served by good transport links. Other factors which must not be minimized are those of the Dutch farming community's initiative and commercial acumen and the development of an efficient system of markets and co-operative farming schemes.

Arable farming

Much arable production in the Netherlands is geared to the needs of livestock feeding but cereals (wheat and barley) are also grown for human needs. High yields are characteristic, average yields being $4\frac{1}{2}$ tons per hectare for wheat, 30 tons per hectare for potatoes and 40 tons per hectare for sugar beet. Nevertheless, home production supplies only about 40 per cent of the country's requirements for stock feeding and a somewhat lower proportion of the cereal needed for human food. Dutch production of potatoes (both as a vegetable and for industrial use in the preparation of starch) is above home requirements and these feature in the export trade. Sugar beet is especially suited to areas of soils based on sea-clay, as in the province of Zeeland. However, the Randstad region produces less than one-fifth of the Dutch totals of sugar beet and potatoes. Cereal grains rank second to grassland, apart from the Harlemmermeer area, where they are dominant.

Cattle and other livestock

Although the main regions of grassland and heavy concentrations of cattle are in the eastern Netherlands, there are considerable areas of this form of farming in the Randstad provinces. The southern region of the Betuwe district is particularly important, as is also the eastern zone between Amsterdam and Utrecht and much of the central area. Milk production for the main centres of population is naturally a major consideration. Pig-rearing and poultry farming is also represented, leading to areas of mixed livestock farms between Utrecht and Rotterdam in particular (Fig. 6).

Since dairying is such an important branch of Dutch agriculture, it is worth examining briefly some of the characteristics of this activity. The total number of cattle continues to rise annually and in 1970 stood at 4 366 000 compared with 4 116 000 two years earlier. This included calves for fattening as well as milk-producing cattle. The western provinces account for approximately one-fifth of this total.

Although grassland is the main source of food for Dutch livestock and accounts for nearly 62 per cent of the total agricultural land-use, it can only be used for grazing between approximately late April and November. In addition, some twenty per cent of the grass crop is used for haymaking and a further ten per cent goes to silage. Where mixed farming is practised (as in much of the Randstad) a slightly higher percentage of grassland is used for grazing since arable production provides beet and turnips for winter feed.

Dutch cattle farming is primarily geared to the production of butter and cheese and a high milk yield per cow is therefore required. The 1970 average production of 4340 kg per cow is amongst the world's highest and includes a high average butterfat content. In addition to quantity of output, quality is carefully controlled by a government inspection service for all dairy products. The dairy industry is an old established one in the Netherlands but today it is no longer made up of small individual producers and is run on almost a factory basis. These large units are privately run but are organized by co-operatives, each of which has a national organization to maintain standards and also to protect the commercial interests of the industry.

In addition to milk, cheese, cream, and butter production, milk powder (for export to tropical areas), whey (for livestock feeding), and condensed milk are also produced. The Netherlands is the world's chief cheese-exporting country but only fourth in terms of export of butter (after New Zealand, Denmark, and Australia). The Netherlands are also amongst the world's largest producers of margarine, based largely on the import of vegetable oil seeds.

Size of agricultural holdings

The size and layout of agricultural holdings in the Randstad varies according to such factors as the type of farming and the natural features of the district. The historical development of the particular area is a further factor. Thus, recently reclaimed polder lands have regular fields and farm sizes whilst other areas exhibit the pattern of irregular and small fields common to much West European agriculture. A scattered pattern of fields belonging to the individual landholder also exists in the Netherlands but progress in the consolidation of fields and farming is proceeding, having been under way since 1924. In the Netherlands as a whole there are still over one million hectares of land to be considered for farm consolidation but the three western provinces contribute a proportionately smaller part. Figures for 1968 show that 30 000 hectares in the west have been reallocated but there are at least 200 000 hectares still to be reorganized. An additional special problem of this region is the need for preliminary water control schemes.

Clearly, however, land holdings for many horticultural activities are necessarily small. Nursery cultivation and glasshouses require only a matter of a few hectares to provide an economic livelihood. Thus, the bulb fields of the Netherlands, occupying (1970) some 12 365 hectares produce 284 million guilders worth of crops—i.e. nearly 23 000 guilders per hectare annually—much of which is for export. To obtain a similar value of production from, say, sugar beet under an intensive system of agriculture would still require about ten times as much land.

5 Industries

As has already been outlined, the industrial areas of the Randstad, although scattered throughout the region, show two marked belts of concentration. These are the Amsterdam–North Sea and the Rotterdam–Europoort zones.

The power basis for Dutch industry today is oil (Table 2)—mainly imported but including also a small quantity from the home field. An increasingly important source of power is supplied by home-produced natural gas, from the Groningen field in particular, via a network of pipelines running throughout the country. The earlier power source was coal, some of which was supplied by the Limburg coalfield, currently in the process of closure, creating problems of readjustment not unlike those of other European coalfields. The supplies of coal/coke required by the Hoogovens industry at IJmuiden (below) today come from abroad, and from the U.S.A. in particular. A small proportion of electricity is also supplied from the nuclear power station at Petten in North Holland province.

Other factors in Dutch industrial development relate to the national economy and international trade, shipping, and agriculture. The recent development of international concerns which had their origins in the Netherlands, associated with such individuals as Anton Philips, Van den Bergh, Jurgens, Hartogh, and Stork, can be considered a modern example of the Dutch commercial enterprise which enabled this small country to become prosperous in medieval times. Although lacking in many natural resources the Dutch have been able to develop industries to a high level based on little more than the mainly agricultural raw materials of their country. Current importance of coastal sites for large-scale industrial development has further enhanced the value of main waterways leading to these sites. The import of oil and the resulting growth of refineries and petrochemical industries along the New Waterway west of Rotterdam is a major factor of industrial location here. Similarly, the need for imported supplies has helped the growth of industry along the North Sea Canal leading to Amsterdam. Sites for further industrial development and expansion of existing industries are therefore earmarked in both these areas and also where additional reclamation from the sea may be feasible (e.g. Maasvlakte, west of Europoort). It must also be remembered that, over a period of several centuries, the Dutch have been involved in international trade, shipping, and the development of overseas countries, particularly in the tropics. These links have produced materials for industrial development (e.g. tropical foods for processing in Europe) as well as the stimulus for such development.

Iron and steel

The traditional form of heavy industry—that of iron and steel production—is primarily represented by the Royal Netherlands Blast Furnaces and Steelworks at Velsen near IJmuiden. The Dutch name for this complex is Hoogovens, and included with this integrated steel plant are six blast furnaces and rolling mills producing plates, tubes, and wide strip sheet steel, as well as rods, reinforcing steel, and tinplate. Limited and specialized steelworks are also to be found at

TABLE 2
Dutch power resources 1970
(To facilitate comparison all figures are expressed in units of a million million calories)

	Oil	Hard Coal	Natural Gas
Production	19 186	30 335	266 844
Imports	745 702	40 100	—
Exports	387 805	21 507	95 191
Home consumption*	299 808	47 937	168 613

*Excluding bunkerage and losses in production etc.

TABLE 3
Dutch production of iron and steel

	(million kg)			
	1958	1963	1968	1970
Pig iron	917	1 078	2 821	3 594
Steel ingots	1 419	2 324	3 689	5 011

Delft (steel cable manufacture) and Utrecht (associated with the railway workshops).

Total Dutch steel production has shown a pattern of continuing increase but the Netherlands are net importers of iron and steel. The raw materials of the industry are also largely imported into the Netherlands so that the coastal location of Hoogovens is important. Ore comes from Sweden, Spain, North Africa, and Canada; nearly half the coke total is imported (1972) from the United States, the remainder coming from Belgium, Germany and a decreasing amount from the Limburg field.

The need to import materials need not be seen as a problem in the overall European context. Of greater concern is the relatively small scale of the industry compared with other European units of production. It is perhaps significant therefore that Hoogovens have recently entered into an agreement with the German firm of Hoesch which may eventually lead to the building of a second iron and steel works at Europoort.

Oil and chemicals

Oil refining and associated petrochemical developments are concentrated in the Rotterdam–Europoort region, where they have contributed to a rapidly developing industrial scene during the 1960s. In addition to this, Rotterdam is Europe's leading port in volume of freight handled, catering for an extensive hinterland with cargo of great variety. Transit trade in 1970 accounted for over 65 million tons in the Rotterdam area whilst Amsterdam handled some 12 million tons of goods in transit through the Netherlands.

The New Waterway, which links Rotterdam with the North Sea, dates from 1871 and, although it requires continual dredging, it is one of the busiest routes for sea traffic in the world. The first growth areas in the Rotterdam region after about 1870 were on the southern side of the Nieuwe Maas with city extensions and harbour construction in the areas of Rotterdam South, Koningshaven, Binnenhaven, Rijnhaven, Maashaven, and Waalhaven. Pernis became the first locality for petroleum harbour development (between 1929 and 1936) and in 1947 construction work began at Botlek, further downstream. The massive additional extension at the entrance to the New Waterway, together with reclamation from the North Sea (the Maasvlaakte) began in 1958. In 1966, dredging was started to allow tankers of more than 200 000 tons to enter the port. The petrochemical complex covers the greater part of the land within the harbour area and includes five refineries (B.P., Gulf, Shell, Esso, Chevron), associated chemical works, storage areas, and pipeline terminals. These pipelines cater for national trade (to the Mobil refinery near Amsterdam) and also for international supplies to Belgium (Antwerp) and via Limburg to the Ruhr.

Products associated with the Dutch chemical industry include fertilizers, carbide, plastics, disinfectants, medicines, synthetic fibres, cosmetics, and paint. There is probably a greater variety of final products made in other parts of the Randstad and the Netherlands in general, but the raw materials may well be obtained from this New Waterway complex. In addition to the firms with refineries here other internationally acknowledged firms, such as I.C.I., have important factories. Unilever and Philips are probably the best known Dutch-based industrial groups but within the chemical industry the Dutch firms also include Koninklijke Zout (national salt concern) and Hoogovens (above) as well as the State coal-mining interest, Staatsmijn. The chemical industry in general has shown a spectacular pattern of growth in the two decades since 1950. Turnover in 1950 was 1190 million guilders (about £130 million) but this had more than quadrupled by 1960 and in 1970 had reached 13 842 million guilders (more than £1600 million) to become the third most important industry in the Netherlands judged by turnover.

Even so, this figure is little more than half that of the Dutch metal industry (including shipbuilding) which in 1970 had a turnover of 25 464 million guilders. In second place in 1970 came the industries associated with food, drink, and tobacco with 23 421 million guilders. These

TABLE 4
Manufacturing industries in order of importance, by groups of industry, for the main towns of the Randstad

Town/municipality	Food, beverages, tobacco	Oil, petrol, rubber, and chemicals	Metal products	Textiles	Machinery	Electrical	Basic metal industries	Building materials	Paper	Clothing, leather, etc.	Transport equipment	Printing, publishing, etc.
Amsterdam	4				5					1	2	3
Rotterdam	1	2	5	4							3	
The Hague	3		5	4		2						1
Utrecht	2				5	3					1	4
Velsen	2	3	5				1		4			
Haarlem	2			4						5	3	1
Schiedam	2	5	3					4			1	
Delft	3	1		5		2					4	
Leiden	3			2	1						4	5
Hilversum			4	2	5	1						3

Based on Atlas of the Netherlands and data from 1963 General Economic Census.

Note: Only the first five groups of industries for each port have been recorded in this classification and no account is taken of exact or relative sizes of industry.

figures are of course for the whole country and do not refer to the Randstad alone. Nevertheless, there are major concentrations of these latter industries in the western Netherlands so that approximately one-half of the Dutch workers in the metal and shipbuilding industries work here and a similar fraction of those concerned with food, beverages, and tobacco are also employed here. Two-thirds of the country's workers in the chemical industry are employed in the western Netherlands. Of the total industrial population in the Netherlands nearly 40 per cent work in the three western provinces (469 000 out of 1 179 000 in 1964).

Other industries

A great variety of industries are represented in the Randstad region. The twelve main groups, as represented by the five most important in each of the largest towns of the area are shown in the accompanying Table 4. The food, beverages, and tobacco group occurs in all but one case with machinery and transport equipment also ranking high. The printing and publishing industries also feature prominently on this list and in fact some two-thirds of Dutch employment in these industries is in the Randstad region.

The foregoing discussion has focussed attention on the role of the manufacturing industries in the Randstad. The total working population includes those engaged in a variety of other occupations. These include the whole range of service industries including retail and wholesale distribution, public utilities, commerce, banking and insurance, transport and communications. The total employed population of Amsterdam exceeds 380 000, of whom little more than one-third are involved in the manufacturing sector previously described. Similar figures obtained in the Rotterdam area where the employed population totalled some 309 000 in 1964, whilst in The Hague only about one-quarter of some 250 000 workers were employed in industrial occupations *per se*.

6 Population

The fundamental problems in a densely peopled area such as Randstad Holland are linked with the human element: the actual numbers of people in the area, what they do, their prosperity and needs for employment, food, and leisure. The problems may be referred to in general terms as population pressures, and they give rise to consideration of such terms as 'over-population' and 'optimum' future population. Where the geographical area concerned is relatively limited in size and has limited resources, as is clearly the case in the Randstad, then the population factors assume considerable significance for they affect patterns of employment, housing, recreation, food production, and travel.

Distribution and density

A basic knowledge of this most dynamic factor of all, namely population size, distribution, and possible growth patterns, is therefore required at this point. It is well known that the Netherlands as a whole is the most densely populated of the Western European countries, with a figure of 389 people per square kilometre for the whole country in 1970. The actual towns, of course, exhibit a much higher population density with central areas often having well in excess of 100 inhabitants per hectare. The average overall figure for those municipalities which comprise the Randstad is 2563 persons per square kilometre. Actual population figures for the seventy municipalities comprising the urbanized Randstad, as numbered on Fig. 1, are given in the Appendix, and the ten Randstad agglomerations are listed in Table 5.

The average annual percentage increase in population for the Netherlands which was running at 1·35 per cent in 1965 had declined to 1·25 per cent in late 1970, but this still suggests a population increase by the year 2000 from the present figure of 13 million to something in the order of 18 million. The latter represents a reduction from the figure of about 20 million used by the Dutch Government Second Report on Physical Planning (1966), and a recent Statistical Yearbook of the Netherlands gave a figure of only 17+ million as the A.D. 2000 estimate.

At the present time approximately 46·2 per cent of the total Dutch population lives in the three western provinces of North Holland, South Holland, and Utrecht, but as these provinces account for little more than 20 per cent of the total surface area of the Netherlands (page 8) it is clear that population densities are very high. A further feature of the pattern of population distribution in the whole country is the concentration in towns: 92 per cent of the entire

TABLE 5
Randstad agglomerations with 100 000 inhabitants and over
(1 January 1971)

	Central Municipality	Other Municipalities of the Agglomeration	Total
Amsterdam	820 406	215 593	1 035 999
Rotterdam	679 032	387 145	1 066 177
The Hague	537 643	172 885	710 528
Utrecht	278 417	181 053	459 470
Haarlem	172 612	66 637	239 249
Leiden	100 135	64 616	164 751
Dordrecht/	100 935		
Zwijndrecht	32 412	38 494	171 841
Hilversum	98 948	15 914	114 862
Velsen/	67 501		
Beverwijk (IJmond)	41 029	29 354	137 884
Zaanstreek	65 981	64 986	130 967
			4 231 728

population at the beginning of 1971 living in municipalities of more than 5000 people and 31 per cent of the entire population in the large municipalities of more than 100 000 population. The Randstad thus exemplifies Dutch urban concentration at its most marked.

The present population of the Randstad (1970) totals approximately 5·7 million and it seems likely that this will increase to around 8 million by the year 2000. Room for houses, services, and communications will thus be required for the extra 2 300 000—as well as jobs. Land-use implications regarding loss of agricultural land, and the problem of planning for this increased number with no major change in existing characteristics of the Randstad, i.e. retention of the greenheart, are considered in the chapter dealing with planning (pages 39–43).

Population characteristics

If the overall characteristics of the Randstad population were to be summarized it might be said that this area is characterized by young, mobile, prosperous, and town-dwelling inhabitants. The fact that over most of the area there is a lower percentage than the national average of inhabitants aged over 65 suggests the fact that this is a youthful working population and the patterns of commuter travel and car-owning statistics confirm the contention that here is a mobile population. Figures for job-holding and changes in employment are not available but since well over half the total employed are engaged in service occupations of the tertiary sector it would seem realistic to consider this population to be mobile in the employment sense also. Further, wages for all categories of work (skilled, semi-skilled, and unskilled) are higher in the Randstad and particularly in North and South Holland provinces. The largest group of tax-payers in the highest income-bracket (based on 1958 figures of at least 100 000 guilders per annum) are to be found in the towns of the Randstad, and the greatest proportion of taxpayers with personal property of at least 200 000 guilders value (1964) live here. In the last-named case the major concentration is in The Hague/Scheveningen area.

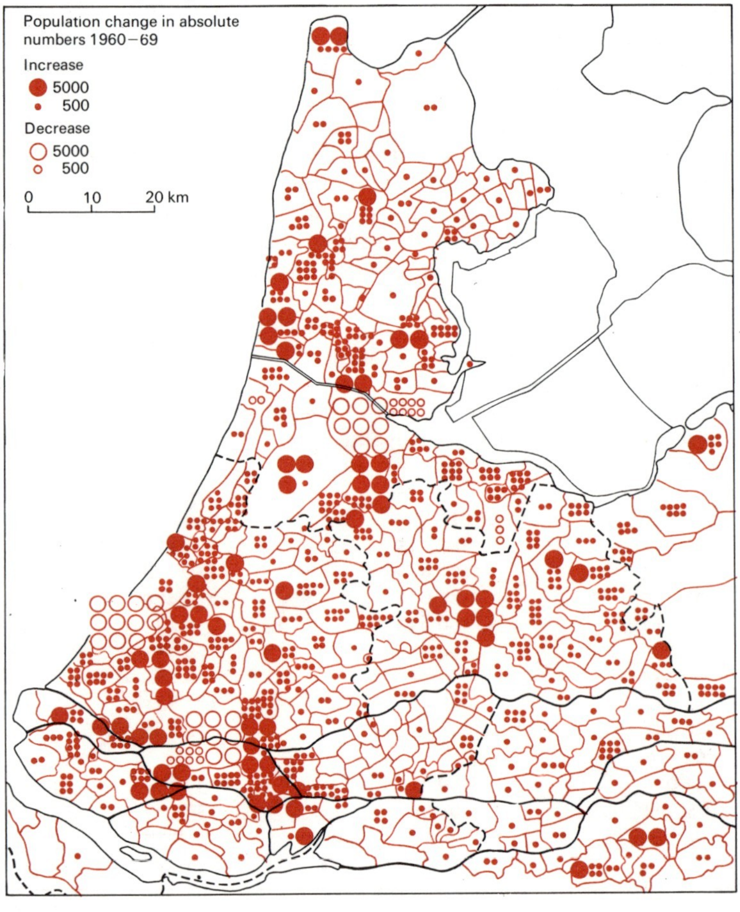

Fig. 7a. Population change, 1960–9, in the Randstad area by absolute numbers per municipality (after Tamsma in *T.E.S.G.*, 1971)

The agglomerations defined in Table 5 consist of the central municipality (named) together with contiguous suburban areas. Twenty-one such agglomerations are listed in the Netherlands Statistical Yearbook and the ten in the table are within the Randstad area defined previously. From the standpoint of world population growth it can be noted that the recent average annual increase in population in the Netherlands is at a higher rate than that of many of her neighbours. Over the period 1963–8 the mean rate for Dutch population increase was 1·3 per cent. This compares with the following figures:

Belgium	0·7 per cent
France	0·9 per cent
Italy	0·8 per cent
United Kingdom	0·6 per cent
West Germany	0·9 per cent
U.S.A.	1·2 per cent
U.S.S.R.	1·1 per cent

As we have seen, however, there are signs that this national trend may be changing. The natural increase in population (excess of live births over deaths) had fallen to 0·99 per cent for the period 1969 to 1970 and the major influxes of people from overseas have stopped. These were the result of the independence of the Dutch East Indies (Indonesia) and the repatriation of many Dutch nationals in the early 1960s and also of the internal movements of labour within the E.E.C. in its earlier years.

Despite this more hopeful sign, migration of population within the Netherlands has tended to aggravate the population pressures on the western provinces, at least until very recently. The drift to the town tended to be accentuated in these areas and was also accompanied by a movement to the prosperous west. As is shown in Fig. 7 the pattern in the Randstad is now overwhelmingly one of population movements to the suburban municipalities. Although some of these people may in fact be total newcomers to the area, it is more likely that this outward expansion consists of former city-dwellers and their population growth.

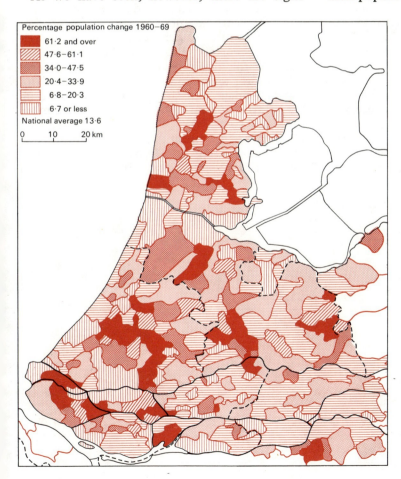

Fig. 7b. Population change, 1960–9, in the Randstad area as percentage of the 1960 figures (after Tamsma in *T.E.S.G.*, 1971)

7 Towns and Urbanization

The map of the Netherlands is clearly dominated by the many towns of the Randstad. This ring of towns is in fact better and more accurately called a crescent since it is not fully complete in the south-east. In the south-west a group of towns form a 'Little Ring' surrounding agricultural land: these include the towns of The Hague, Leiden, Alphen, Gouda, Rotterdam, and Delft. The Randstad crescent or ring of towns is most nearly complete in the north, from east of Utrecht through Hilversum and Amsterdam to Haarlem.

Town growth

Most of the main centres of the Randstad are towns of considerable age and were well established by 1600. With the creation of the separate Kingdom of the Netherlands in 1645 town development in the provinces of Holland entered a phase of expansion and consolidation in the form of many more permanent buildings. However, some form of political stability had existed in at least the western Netherlands since the fourteenth century and many towns owed their origin to trading and other economic activities of the medieval period. In addition to the necessity for protection from water inundation, involving the creation of dry sites for towns, it was necessary in the latter part of the sixteenth century to design fortified towns or to improve the defensive possibilities of existing towns, for this was the period of war against the Spanish. The combination of military defence and water defence with moats, bastions, walls, and dikes is now a scenic feature of towns both large and small in the Randstad. The seventeenth century, by contrast, was one of peace, and town improvements and extensions were marked by the building of guild halls, churches, and market places, the straightening of canals, and the evolution of many town cores still extant. Wooden buildings and thatch were prohibited by law in these central areas and hence architectural styles in brick and stone became established. This was the Renaissance, the Golden Period in Dutch civilization and town-building.

During the succeeding centuries, developments were associated with the consolidation, or filling-in, of the urban structure and it was not until the mid-nineteenth century with the appearance of railways on the Dutch scene that any major change occurred. Problems then arose: for example the existence of an already compact urban core, together with the complications of water drainage and the difficulties of building heavy structures on soft, low-lying ground made necessary some 1600 piles for the construction of Amsterdam Central station on the north side of the pre-existing city. In nearly every town in the Randstad the railway station is placed

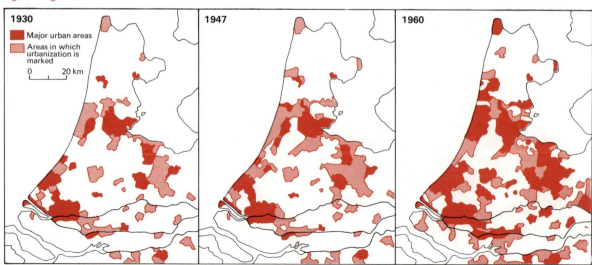

Fig. 8. Stages in urbanization

Recent housing developments on the outskirts of Amsterdam KLM Aerocarto

eccentrically to the urban core and frequently just beyond the town wall or town dike. Later industrial extensions to the Randstad towns continued to be compact because of physical constraints, and the sprawling town did not appear on the Dutch scene until well into the twentieth century.

The outward growth of the many towns in the Randstad became apparent around the middle of the twentieth century. The pattern of urbanized municipalities in 1930, 1947, and 1960 which forms Fig. 8 makes this quite clear. The dangers likely to attend future growth of this kind are evident on the last of these maps and are also shown by the population growth patterns in Figs. 11 and 12 on pp. 40–1.

Urbanization

Urbanization may be defined as the development of the town characteristics of housing, population densities, and occupations. By implication this development is one which replaces a pre-existing rural scene. In its simplest form, urban development can be recognized by the mere presence of built-up areas—residential housing, shopping areas and other amenities, industrial activities on various scales and similar land utilization. The presence of such aspects can be clearly recognized on the ground and also on air photographs and maps.

Nevertheless, most of these characteristics can be found in a truly rural landscape and indeed many of them are necessary for the continuation of life in these areas. A more precise definition of urbanization is therefore required. One such definition has been used for the depiction of the municipalities in Fig. 8. This is a combination of total population numbers with population density expressed in terms of persons per square kilometre and it is referred to as 'morphological urbanization'. This definition offers the advantage of quick calculation from municipality data, the local authority of the municipality being the smallest administrative unit in the Netherlands.

Another definition of urbanization is a socio-economic one, where the occupation structure of the population is considered. This can also be worked out for the statistical unit of the municipality in the Netherlands. Urban occupations as against agrarian ones can then be used as a method of distinguishing the degree of urbanization; e.g. $>$ 90 per cent of the economically active male population not engaged in agriculture, fishing, or hunting indicates a highly urbanized community.

The seventy Randstad municipalities shown in Fig. 1 are characterized by the following set of criteria for the working male population:

$<$ 20 per cent in agriculture, fishing, and hunting
$>$ 25 per cent in industrial occupations
$>$ 11 per cent in shops and trade
$>$ 6 per cent in transport industries

Population change

The rapid spread of urbanization can also be depicted as suburbanization, as increasing mobility of the population has enabled the towns to spread outwards at relatively low densities of development. In many cases this has been accompanied by a decline in the population of the central areas of towns. This can be seen for

Amsterdam, Rotterdam, and The Hague in Fig. 7, showing the changes in population over the period 1960–9, in both absolute numbers and in relative terms.

It is possible to recognize three types of urban areas on the basis of population change over recent years. First, there are the central areas of the large urban agglomerations, usually consisting of one large single municipality such as Amsterdam, Rotterdam, or The Hague. Surrounding these are the suburban fringe municipalities—the 'other municipalities of the agglomeration' of Table 5. Finally there are the municipalities of various sizes which make up the open middle region or greenheart of the Randstad. These are not included within the seventy municipalities comprising the urbanized Randstad (Fig. 1) but are clearly much affected by activities in the surrounding areas.

Population in the urban core municipalities is now declining but between 1960 and 1966 it had increased by a mere 1·3 per cent (Steigenga, 1968) whereas during this same earlier period the 'other municipalities' grew by 18 per cent. The average growth figure for areas *outside the urban agglomerations*—the open central region of the Randstad—at this same time was the disquietingly high figure of 10·7 per cent. In this latter figure, in particular, lies the key to some of the most serious problems with which the planners of the Randstad are faced at the present day.

It can be concluded from this account, and from the map of population changes over the period 1960–9 (Fig. 7), that regional plans to limit suburbanization are somewhat illusory as (a) slight increases have been allowed by the provincial authorities to the populations of former rural villages and (b) many local authorities in the middle region of the Randstad have encouraged growth.

Hierarchical relationships

The Randstad towns can be relatively easily classified in terms of population size and, as shown in Fig. 2, their agglomerations can be

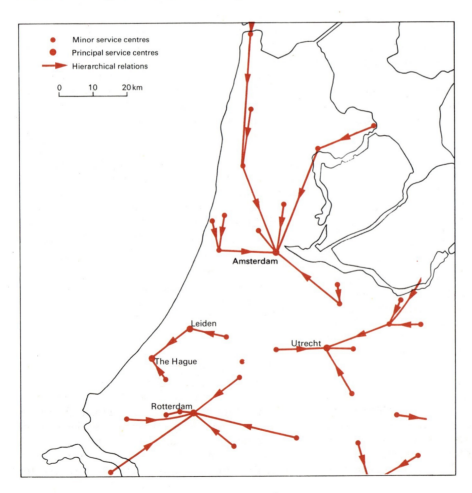

Fig. 9a. Urban hierarchies (after Keuning, 1964)

combined to present a picture of several major urban units. Of these it is clear that Amsterdam and Rotterdam are overwhelmingly the largest, with The Hague and Utrecht next in significance. Although the remaining large agglomerations can then be ranked in order by population size, a number of additional municipalities—the population of which generally lies between 50 000 and 100 000 at the present time—are also significant as central places.

Various representations of the hierarchical relationships between these urban centres have been made and one such study forms the basis for Fig. 9a. The relationships between most of the minor and the five major centres are shown here by a system of arrows, which illustrate the direction of allegiance, or hierarchical order. The major centres in this scheme are Amsterdam, Rotterdam, The Hague, Utrecht, and Leiden (Keuning, 1964).

A more recent theoretical consideration of the relationships between the principal towns of the Randstad (Buursink, 1971) recognizes the following pattern based on the existence of some key institutions such as schools, hospitals, and newspaper offices (Fig. 9b).

Primary centres: Alkmaar, Haarlem, Amsterdam, The Hague, Utrecht, Rotterdam, Dordrecht.

Secondary centres: Amersfoort, Zaandam, Hilversum, Leiden, Gouda, Gorinchem.

Third order centres are quite numerous in this classification and in the three provinces include the following:

Zeist, Woerden, Culemborg;
Purmerend, Bussum;
Hoorn, Den Helder, Enkhuizen, Schagen;
Beverwijk, Velsen;
Delft, Alphen (a/d Rijn);
Vlaardingen, Schiedam, Middelharnis, Oud Beijerland, Spijkenisse and Brielle.

This theoretical pattern implies rigid steps between the three classes but it is emphasized in the study that there is really a continuum between the various centres. The actual population totals for the municipalities involved can be found in the Appendix.

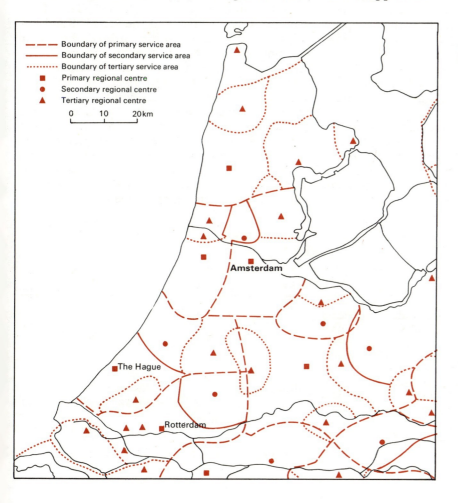

Fig. 9b. Urban hierarchies (after Buursink, 1971)

8 Transport and Communications

The location of the Randstad region of the Netherlands, and in particular its delta situation, focusses attention on transport links by water—sea, river, and canal. The flat and low-lying terrain of this area make most methods of communication relatively easy to construct, but the piecemeal pattern of reclamation of former bodies of water has resulted in a highly irregular pattern of roadways following, for example, the lines of dikes between polders. Recent developments (post 1960) in the network of communications in this area include pipelines for gas and oil.

Water links

The Randstad is at a major junction for international trade, at an interface between overseas transport by ocean freighters, tankers, and container ships on the one hand and the European internal routes by road, rail, and inland water on the other.

The importance of shipping, both sea-borne and by inland water, national and international, is easily apparent from the figures for freight transport (1970) in Table 6.

There is also a considerable amount of international passenger movement through the seaports and airports of the Netherlands. In the former case this is associated with world-wide shipping routes from Amsterdam and Rotterdam, together with routes crossing the North Sea, particularly from the Hook of Holland. In 1970, a total of 1 192 000 passengers arrived at or departed from Dutch sea-ports. Air traffic accounted for considerably more than this, mainly through Schiphol airport where 5 172 000 passengers were handled, but Rotterdam airport also saw some 456 000 passengers that same year. It is interesting to note that all these figures represent considerable increases over the years, there having been only 709 000 shipping arrival and departure passengers in 1963 and 2 000 000 air travellers through the two airports of Amsterdam and Rotterdam that year.

The distinction between internal and external links is particularly important when considering communications by water. The major European seaport is undoubtedly the Rotterdam–Europoort complex described on page 13. The Low Countries as a whole, and the Dutch Randstad in particular, are greatly helped by their position on the North Sea at the mouth of the major Western European rivers, Rhine, Maas, and Scheldt. These rivers are all easily navigable and provide convenient routes from the industrial complexes of the E.E.C. countries, particularly West Germany, to the outside world. Hence the Dutch seaports serve vital roles as European ports and whilst some 45 per cent of inwards and outwards freight movements represent national imports and exports, the remaining 55 per cent are accounted

TABLE 6
Freight transport through the Netherlands 1970
(million tons)

Sea-borne shipping	unloaded	202·7	Railways	national	11·5
	loaded	63·9		international	15·2
	total	266·6		total	26·7
International inland shipping	unloaded	42·9	Road transport	national	175·0
	loaded	81·4		international	33·2
	transit	24·5			
	total	148·8		total	208·2
National inland shipping	total	92·7	Oil pipeline removals	total	24·5

32

Rotterdam—Europoort, looking east

for by international transhipments and distribution. This same feature is also illustrated by the statistics of the inland waterways where more than 70 per cent of the ton–km handled by ships and barges represents international trade. Nevertheless, this still leaves a considerable total quantity of freight to be moved around the Netherlands, and within the Randstad there is a complex pattern of canals and canalized rivers. Most of these are linked with the Rhine traffic which follows the Waal to Dordrecht, thence to the Nieuwe Maas at Rotterdam and the New Waterway to Europoort and the open sea.

Segregation of inland and open sea traffic is now possible in this area, the main Europoort inland water docks being associated with the Hartel canal and thence via the Oude Maas to Dordrecht (Fig. 1). Sea-going traffic is also separated into two main groups. The New Waterway continues to cater for a great variety of shipping but the larger tankers and bulk carriers use the deep-water channel (up to 20 metres) of the Caland Canal. This runs parallel to the New Waterway downstream from Rozenburg and serves various oil and other transhipping harbours as well as the future industrial site at Maasvlakte. A considerable volume of traffic (up to 50 million tons per year) makes use of the existing canal links between Antwerp and the Rotterdam area whilst the third most important canal route, in terms of annual tonnage handled, is that between IJmuiden,

33

Amsterdam Harbour Authority

Above: the Amsterdam–Rhine canal. In addition to the main distributaries of the Rhine and the many drainage canals which cross the Randstad, several important canals provide communications with the area's hinterland. Of these the Amsterdam–Rhine canal is of considerable significance and has been constantly improved to allow for successively larger barge traffic. The variety and amount of traffic is indicated in this view, which shows the extremely low-lying nature of the adjacent land. Note the protective dike on the right.

Below: dual carriageways on the outskirts of Amsterdam

Amsterdam Harbour Authority

Amsterdam and Utrecht. Two principal canals are involved in this latter case—the North Sea Canal and the Amsterdam–Rhine canal. Comparatively recent improvements to the latter include a new section at the junction with the Rhine to make this turn easier for larger shipping. Other improvements to this canal are still in progress and should be completed by 1980. The problem is one of accommodating a continually growing amount of traffic, and new ideas and investment are constantly required in order to maintain the lead over other European ports.

Roads

The Dutch network of main roads serving the principal towns is well established and in terms of kilometres per square kilometre of land is the densest in Western Europe. Nevertheless, the rapid increase in the number of motor vehicles, together with the expansion of the urban areas, a higher standard of living, and demands for personal transport have made it necessary for the authorities to re-appraise the road network (see below, page 35).

The existing dual carriageways of motorway standard in the Randstad link together Utrecht–Amsterdam, Amsterdam–The Hague–Rotterdam, and The Hague–Utrecht. Additionally, Rotterdam and Utrecht are linked by motorway via Gouda. There is, therefore, no direct motorway route between Rotterdam and Amsterdam, but such a route would, of course, lead directly across the greenheart of the Randstad consuming much land and adding to the urbanized nature of the landscape.

Urban motorways, connected with ring routes and/or major road tunnels beneath the IJ and the Nieuwe Maas have recently been completed. Nevertheless the central areas of all the major cities are still highly congested with traffic throughout most days and particularly during the 'travel to work or home' rush hours of morning, midday, and evening.

Particularly impressive features of Dutch motorway building in recent years have been the construction of various road-tunnels: in addition to those mentioned above there is also the Schiphol airport route which takes the Amsterdam–The Hague motorway beneath a main runway and a taxiing area. Roundabout intersections on motorways also include flyovers and traffic control by lights; the resulting use of land is therefore quite high and a main crossroad can take 10 hectares of land or more—this in an urban region where open space is a precious commodity.

Road transport is the principal means of internal freight movement within the Randstad despite the large volume carried on the Dutch canal system (Table 6). Goods traffic on the roads has more than doubled since 1958 in the Netherlands as a whole but passenger vehicles are increasing in number at an even greater rate. Use of public transport, measured in passenger-kilometres, has remained relatively static at about 18 000 million per annum over the last two decades.

Passenger transport in the Netherlands is increasingly by car (private car registrations in 1959 were only 456 500, in 1970 well over 2 million). Car travel for the whole country had reached 75 700 million passenger-kilometres per annum by 1969 and is still increasing. The motor-bicycle has decreased in importance and the typical Dutch upright bicycle with 'balloon' tyres has been ousted by the auto-cycle (10 600 million passenger-kilometres in 1969). Figures for private car registrations by provinces in the Netherlands show the overwhelming dominance of the Randstad area, the three western provinces accounting for more than half the total. The other side to this picture is of course the pressing need for adequate roads and the ever-present likelihood of traffic congestion. In relation to this latter consideration one must also bear in mind the role of the Dutch as carriers of international road freight.

Railways

A complex network of railways exists in the Randstad area, but it is principally located around the periphery of the area. The original main line of the system ran from Amsterdam to Haarlem and on to The Hague and Rotterdam. The Hague has a direct link, via Gouda, with Utrecht and this line runs from a separate station (the Staatspoor station) distinct from the through services (Hollandsch Spoor). Here is a reminder that the railway lines in this country originated in a variety of separate routes which over a period of nearly a century and a half grew to make up the present network. Dutch railways have been organized on a national basis since 1937 and extensive electrification has resulted in the network having the highest proportion of electrified lines in Europe.

Railways throughout the country, but especially in the Randstad, are primarily concerned with passenger traffic. A frequent service of fast trains between the main cities is supplemented by local stopping trains, also at frequent intervals, but the suburban stations are noticeably fewer

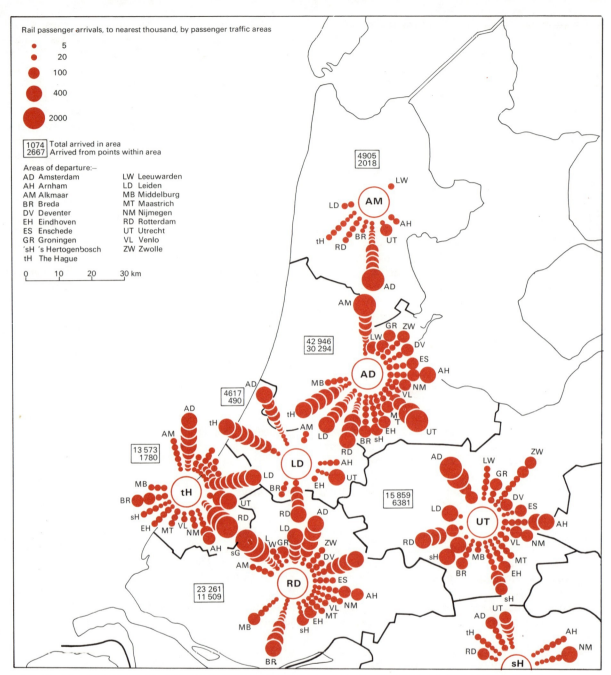

Fig. 10. Passenger commuter traffic by rail in the Randstad area (based on 1959 survey, after *T.E.S.G.,* 1962)

TABLE 7
Time by intercity trains between main Randstad centres

Amsterdam–Haarlem	13 minutes
Amsterdam–The Hague	41 minutes
Amsterdam–Hilversum	25 minutes
Amsterdam–Utrecht	31 minutes
Rotterdam–Amsterdam	58 minutes
Rotterdam–Utrecht	34 minutes

in number than on many peripheral areas of cities elsewhere in Europe. The railway lines of the Randstad provide a major means of commuter travel from town to city and, with the various centres being so closely situated, there is a considerable volume of this traffic (Fig. 10).

In nearly every case a fast train with the timing as in Table 7 operates at least once per hour, with slower services one, two, or three times per hour between these fast ones.

Within the main Randstad cities public transport is predominantly by tram or bus. Tramway tracks are in some cases confined to separate sections of roadway or to central sections of boulevards and this makes for a relatively rapid means of conveyance less hindered by other road traffic. Indeed, trams are given a certain degree of priority in the traffic code and at many intersections. The integration of these public transport systems with the railways is apparent in these cities by the close juxtaposition of terminus points and central stations.

An 'underground' railway line (metro) has been in operation in Rotterdam since 1968 and a similar system is under construction in Amsterdam. These too have the respective Central stations as one terminus and in the case of Rotterdam a highly integrated inner suburban interchange has been created to the south of the city at Zuidplein.

Air traffic

The major airport of the Randstad region is also the main Dutch international airport of Schiphol, some 11 kilometres (7 miles) south-west of Amsterdam. Rotterdam's airport similarly lies on the greenheart side of the built-up area, to the north-west of that city, at Zestienhoven. Schiphol is by far the most important of the Dutch airports, handling over 100 000 international flights in 1969 as against nearly 22 000 at Rotterdam. Major international flights include services to North America, but more than 80 per cent of the passengers at Schiphol have a European destination.

Freight transport by air is of lesser significance but, as already mentioned, the fruit and flower trade in which speed to a market is important does make increasing use of this facility. In 1968–9 the freight revenue of K.L.M.* was

*K.L.M. = Koninklijke Luchtvaart Maatschappij, or Royal Dutch Airlines, founded in 1919 with this same name and hence one of the world's oldest established national airways with unchanged title.

74 million guilders but in 1970–1 this had reached 222 million guilders. Passenger and baggage revenue was correspondingly 349 million guilders and 657 million guilders.

Air transport poses particular problems in the Randstad with the pattern of future land needs being difficult to predict. There is a clear clash of interest, for town and airport tend to expand towards each other. The layout of additional runways at Schiphol has been engineered to cause minimum noise disturbance to the suburbs of Amsterdam but it is highly likely that an additional airport will be required in due course. Possibilities which can be considered will almost certainly involve reclaimed land—either within the framework of existing schemes such as that of the Southern IJsselmeer polders or in some new scheme in the North Sea. Inland travel by road and/or rail to such an airport will create new problems no doubt.

Pipelines and powerlines

The main pipelines in the Randstad, other than the traditional ones for water and town gas, are concerned with the distribution of oil and petrochemical products from terminals in the Europoort area (page 23), or with the distribution of natural gas from the Groningen field. In addition, the removal of waste-water and the transfer of semi-manufactured products of the plastics industry both now, and increasingly in the future, must be borne in mind. Large-diameter pipelines bring special problems of construction in an intensely developed area such as the Randstad and, as they are costly to move, can well determine the future patterns of growth along their routes. This is particularly important if the products they carry are in any way dangerous and thus for health reasons the pipelines are initially built well away from built-up areas.

Powerlines carrying the main electric grid in the Netherlands are principally in a network of strength ranging from 50 kV to 220 kV but a new supergrid line, forming part of an international European system, has recently been completed between Amsterdam and Rotterdam, thence running south-eastwards across Limburg to the Aachen region of Germany. The main power stations in the Randstad are at Velsen (associated with the iron and steel works of Hoogovens), Amsterdam, Diemen, Leiden, Utrecht, The Hague, and Rotterdam. Although some of these are oil-burning, the majority have been, or are in process of being, converted to natural gas operation. Formerly coal was the power base.

Future developments in communications in

the Netherlands are particularly connected with the country's role as a transhipping centre. Thus, containers form an increasing percentage of sea-borne traffic and facilities for their handling are available in both the Amsterdam and the Europoort harbour areas. A possible area of extension for container handling facilities lies on the northern side of the New Waterway, some three kilometres inland from the Hook of Holland. Roll-on/roll-off shipping services are also catered for and will be expanded: these are mainly on the Hook of Holland to Harwich route at present.

A section of the Europoort 'tank farm' and refineries complex with the Maasvlakte reclamation area in the distance

Bart Hofmeester, Rotterdam

9 Planning the Solution

General considerations

In planning the future pattern of development in the Randstad, the Dutch authorities are concerned with all the facts of the present situation described before, together with projections as to future growth in such matters as population, industrial activity and transport needs. Additionally, the lines of development for the whole country must be considered, as well as the likely local effects at provincial or municipal level.

The themes which have made up the subject matter of preceding chapters suggest that the Randstad's problems arise primarily from three groups of causes.

Environmental factors—position, drainage, soils.
Population pressures—patterns of growth, town development, related social trends, recreation demands.
Industrial and communication activities—national and local needs.

It is immediately obvious that these causal groups are all closely interrelated, but that by far the most important considerations in the Randstad are the physical controls brought about by the terrain and existing patterns of development on the one hand, and the expanding population of the country together with increasing prosperity on the other hand.

Basic decisions on the pattern of future growth in the whole country are influenced by a desire for uniform national growth so that one area, possibly the west of the country, does not become too densely populated compared with the remainder. Development regions and plans for individual towns throughout the country are designed to prevent this but, nevertheless, the likely pattern of population growth to the year 2000 will be as in Column 2 of Table 8 if trends in the 1960s continue.

Even with increased dispersal of population, as in Column 3, a large proportion of the population will reside in the south and west of the country, i.e. chiefly in the Randstad provinces, North Brabant, etc. The chief areas to be encouraged to develop under such a dispersal plan would be in the North: parts of Overijssel province, the tip of the North Holland province peninsula, the Southern IJsselmeer polders, and the province of Zeeland.

Coupled with the overall trends in population growth considered above, changes in major fields of employment are also likely to occur. Thus the 1966 report by the Dutch government on aspects of physical planning in the Netherlands envisaged a reduction by 1980 of the labour force in agriculture to only 5 per cent of the total employed population, whilst some 54 per cent will be occupied in service activities. The remaining 41 per cent in industry would also mark a slight reduction from the 1964 peak of 42 per cent and would presumably reflect such national factors as the closure of the Limburg coalfield and increased mechanization in industry.

This report continues with the comment that the 'urban residential environment ... will in any case have to be doubled by the year 2000'.

TABLE 8

Possible patterns of population growth
(population in millions)

Part of the Netherlands	Population 1965	Population 2000 Continuing at present trend	Population 2000 With greater dispersal
North	1·3	2·3	3·0
East	2·2	4·0	4·3
West	5·7	8·5 } 13·2	} 11·5
South	2·6	4·7	
South-West	0·3	0·5	0·7
Southern IJsselmeer polders	—	—	0·5
	12·1	20·0	20·0

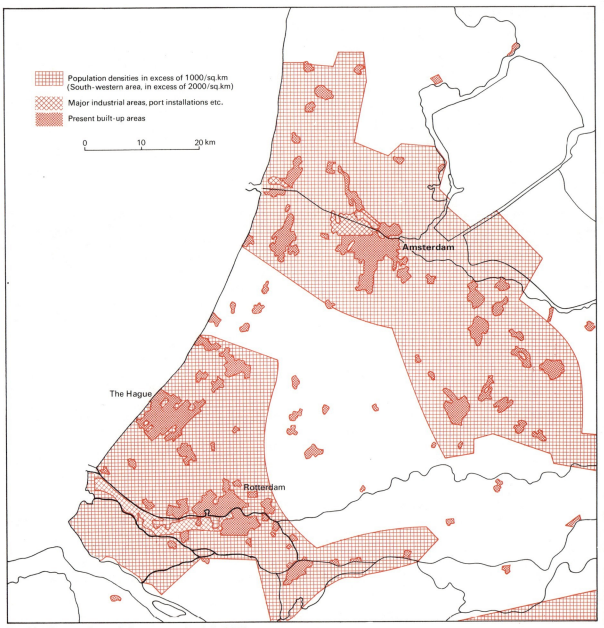

Fig. 11. Expected population pattern by A.D. 2000.

Such enlargement will not mean simply the creation of new towns or the expansion of existing ones but also the provision of new urban facilities and the disappearance of the present-day rural scene from many areas. A corollary of this would be that some existing rural areas would lose their value as recreational regions for the towns.

The Randstad

Let us examine this report as it concerns the Randstad area. The current pattern of a 'ring city' can, as we have seen, be subdivided into a northern residential, industrial, and service zone and a southern counterpart. The northern wing extends from IJmuiden south-eastwards through Amsterdam and on to Utrecht and the southern wing includes The Hague, Delft, Rotterdam, and extends eastwards to Dordrecht (Figs. 2, 3, 4, and 11). The overall density of population in the southern area makes it already the most crowded section of the country. Zones of less developed country extend between these two areas and also south of Rotterdam, approximately

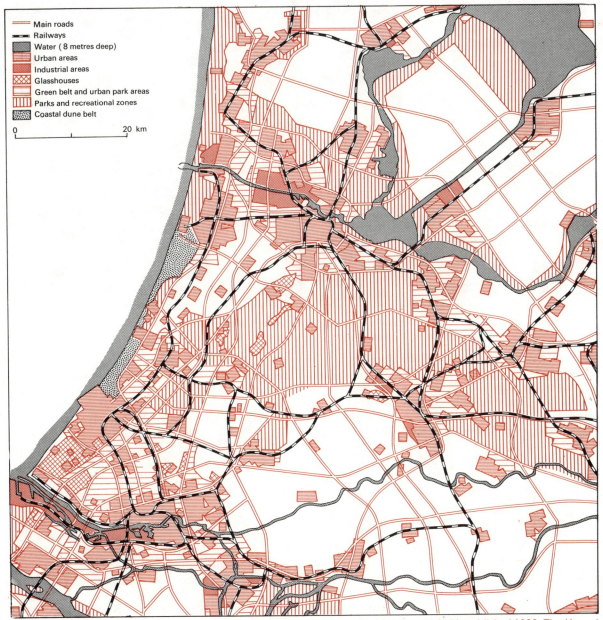

Fig. 12. Proposed pattern of land use, A.D. 2000 (from the Dutch Structure Plan for the year 2000, published 1966, The Hague)

along the line of the river Maas. Southwards again is the series of towns in North Brabant. The principal rural areas and zones available for recreation include the water *plassen* in the centre and east as well as the heathlands along the eastern edge of the Randstad. The western dunes and coastal belt provide an almost continuous fringe of seaside resorts and recreational facilities. It will be remembered that agricultural activities characterize the centre, horticulture the southwest, and of course the newly reclaimed polderlands immediately outside the area to the north-east are also available for agriculture.

The possible pattern of future population distribution in the Netherlands could well continue this twofold wing pattern in the Randstad. There would then result an urbanized zone stretching from the North Sea coast in North Holland through Amsterdam to Utrecht and beyond Arnhem in the east, with population densities averaging between one and two thousand inhabitants per square kilometre. An even more densely peopled area (two thousand per square kilometre and more) would probably characterize

The glasshouse concentration of the Westland area of the Randstad. Notice the tall chimneys carrying waste gasses from the heating plants. Warehouses and loading bays can be seen in the centre of the picture

an area in the south-west of the Randstad, including all that area called the Little Ring earlier in this book (page 28). The North Brabant zone would also show an overall population density similar to those in the northern Randstad. Relatively open 'corridors' of countryside between these three zones would have to be maintained. All these zones would form part of the wider pattern of urban development in Western Europe, this including large sections of Northern Belgium (the Ghent–Brussels–Antwerp triangle), the Paris Region, and North Rhine–Westphalia.

A number of special Randstad characteristics emerge from the plan, the chief among them being the expected disappearance of the clearly defined single town and its replacement either by a city region or by an urban zone. Plans for extensions in one such region affect other areas because of their overlapping spheres of influence.

In the Randstad, continued expansion of population and the demand for new areas to be included in the urban zones are expected to result in developments in a number of 'radiation areas', e.g. North Kennemerland, the Southern IJsselmeer polders, the northern Delta area, and in Gelderland. Between these newly urbanized zones there are to be open spaces which will remain little urbanized, largely agrarian and recreational in character. A number of green belts within the urban zones are designed to act as buffers between the cities. The rural areas serve different functions, particularly where they have attractive scenery and are recognized as being of value as national or local parks, or areas for aquatic sports. Within these park areas there is also a considerable amount of land which can be farmed but the main agrarian districts lie outside the defined zones of Fig. 12.

It is recognized in the 1966 Report on the Physical Planning of the Netherlands that the proposed structural scheme is particularly problematical in the city regions of The Hague and Rotterdam, i.e. the south-western Little Ring. The strong development of the New Waterway port area together with the Rotterdam agglomeration and the vigorous expansion of The Hague as an administrative centre are taking place very close to each other. The important glasshouse concentration of Westland is also in close proximity to these urban growth areas but it, too, has need of land to expand. Office development and government buildings are naturally attracted to The Hague but it is anticipated that the peak period of expansion for these activities is over, and in the case of administrative and research buildings, some decentralization to other parts of the Netherlands is under way.

Administrative organization.

The three provinces of North Holland, South Holland and Utrecht form the main framework in which the Randstad area lies, but as has been shown previously, and as indicated on Fig. 1, the provinces include a great variety of municipalities of all shapes and sizes. The physical planning proposals for the country as a whole have been set out in various government reports and some of the basic themes have been summarized above. The provinces and municipalities have their own planning organizations acting within the framework of the national proposals and, in addition to these various local bodies, there are water control authorities directly answerable to the State.

However, this administrative hierarchy results in a considerable diversity within the country and nowhere is this more acute than in the west. Although there is a great amount of co-operation between all the bodies involved it could possibly be advantageous to have some large groupings of municipalities below the provincial level. A grouping of this kind does exist in the Rotterdam–Europoort area where the Rijnmond public authority groups the municipalities within this extensive harbour area.* A further public body is responsible for the overall policies of the Southern IJsselmeer polders area. Elsewhere in the Randstad a number of municipalities have changed their boundaries since 1960 by annexation of adjacent areas. There are currently plans for co-operation in administration for the Amsterdam–Amstelveen–Haarlemmermeer area; and a southern section of the Randstad greenheart centred on Gouda and extending nearly to Leiden in the west, Utrecht in the east, and adjoining the Rijnmond authority area in the south-west is also planning administrative links.

Major projects

In order that the main outlines of the pattern of future development can be established, State (or central) government and local (provincial and municipal) government projects must be co-ordinated. Large hydraulic projects such as the Southern IJsselmeer polders and the Delta Plan form tangible examples of integrated national schemes. Policies for house-building, agrarian structure, industrialization and provision of social and cultural facilities are all involved in such big developments.

In addition to the reclamation schemes, government projects are concerned with traffic and transportation. For example, in the realm of waterways they involve the upgrading of the other main routes from the Netherlands to Germany (Amsterdam–Germany, Scheldt–Germany) to that of the Rotterdam–Germany standard, enabling pushboats to be used. Road developments involve the construction of a number of new roads, particularly by-pass routes around Amsterdam and Rotterdam, as well as ones linking with the European trunk roads system. For railways, the plan emphasizes modernization and the construction of lines to aid urban communications. Special cases that may be cited as examples here are the construction of a metro line for Rotterdam (now operating between Central Station and Pendrecht; to be extended westwards to Hoogvliet) and for Amsterdam. The latter is now under construction and will initially provide a link between the city centre and Bijlmermeer, the neighbourhood south of Amsterdam currently being built to provide new housing for the city (page 11).

Main line railway routes under discussion include those made possible and desirable by the Southern IJsselmeer polders scheme and the Delta Plan. Detailed reports on a more direct railway line between Amsterdam and The Hague are also available. The present route via Haarlem was opened in 1837 and was the first Dutch railway. It was constructed before the reclamation of the Haarlemmermeer. The currently proposed route would pass via Schiphol airport and also provide rapid links here, replacing the somewhat trying road route which at the present time can take the traveller well over one hour from central Amsterdam in busy periods.

In connection with the Southern IJsselmeer polders scheme it is noteworthy that the proposed structure plan for this area shows a rail link between Amsterdam and Lelystad by 1980. Any proposal for additional and nearer overspill areas serving the Amsterdam agglomeration would of course require rapid transit links. The city authorities of Amsterdam have a number of proposals for additional metro lines, for example. These and other railway lines proposed in the national system are considered in the 1970–5 Netherlands railways plan for the future, *Spoor naar 1970* (Utrecht, 1969, in English). These and many other projects require considerable finance and so must be considered carefully against a whole range of other national needs.

* Shaded in figure 1.

10 Conclusion

From the preceding pages it will have become apparent that Randstad Holland is a thriving and prosperous region of Western Europe. This prosperity, accompanied by a very high density of population and concentration of industry, also produces problems. Many of the problems of the Randstad are a consequence of the terrain and the situation of the area. These geographical features, particularly those of location, also bring advantages to the region, but they have contributed to the historical development of the Randstad, which in its turn has produced controls and restraints to current settlement and future development.

In this flat and level landscape, normally below sea-level in altitude, slight rises are of considerable significance. Similarly, the ever-present threat of inundation by water produces a landscape dominated by the need for drainage or water-protection works. The delta situation of Randstad Holland also means that routeways are influenced by the need to cross many water channels or to follow along them. Constructional problems therefore result, but set against this is the fact that the delta concerned is that of one of Western Europe's major rivers, with a vast industrial hinterland. Thus, economic incentives for development outweight the physical drawbacks of this area.

The incentive to reclaim land from former bodies of water within and around the delta has resulted in a gradual emergence of this area as a single land unit. But the process has been slow and piecemeal, with the result that land units, polders, and fields, tend to demarcate features no longer important to the present economic scene. Towns, too, exhibit the importance of factors of their earlier site and although this has generally been one relating to a dike or drainage feature, it may have been related to past economies.

Of equal importance, perhaps even of greater importance, are the problems related to water in the Randstad landscape. Not only is water closely bound up with the terrain features, with drainage works and with dikes, it is also a highly important commodity in such a densely populated area. Water is always required by agricultural, industrial, and domestic users and in the Randstad the two sources of water are ground-water supplies or rivers. Over-pumping of fresh water, reducing the water table, will allow saline water to encroach and possibly contaminate supplies. Sea-water can also penetrate inland along major inlets such as the New Waterway either by 'creep' at river-bed level or when river discharge is low, as in dry summers. River water, too, cannot be regarded as naturally fresh when the rivers in question, the Maas and the Rhine, have flowed for a considerable distance past towns and through industrial areas. Water treatment processes, whilst suitable for one purpose, can be harmful to others, as for example with the fluoridization of the public mains. This same supply is used by the glasshouse horticultural industry and is likely to harm some plants; hence alternative water supplies will be required for this branch of agriculture.

The population growth in the western Netherlands and its effect on the growth of urban areas has already been shown (pages 25–31) and the continued preference of society for living in some form of town with provision of urban facilities lies behind the proposals for physical planning previously outlined. However, this leaves a number of questions for the future. Thus, it is largely guesswork estimating future population totals for any area and even more prophetic to assume the kinds of housing or environment that a future society will demand. Any planning for the future must be on a flexible basis so that changes in technology and human needs can be incorporated. International developments, particularly in the fields of commerce and technology, can have important repercussions on a highly developed and integrated community such as that of the Randstad. For example, fluctuations in industrial demands for oil could affect the entire pattern of development in the port complex at Rotterdam. Similarly, changes in demands and markets for agricultural products could alter the farming pattern in this region.

Industrial problems of the Randstad can be said to follow two main lines. First, there are the siting problems associated with industrial location, such as the availability and transport of raw materials, labour force and employment, location of markets. Secondly, there are the increasingly important side-effects of industrial development, particularly those concerned with the environment and possible pollution. A vast complex based on a fuel such as oil is bound to give rise to special problems but the risks of fire and explosion are carefully safeguarded by a great many controls and fail-safe devices. Possibly one of the most likely sources of catastrophe is that arising from the transport of large quantities of crude oil in quarter-million-ton tankers. Oil pollution in much smaller amounts is possible not only through the contamination of water supplies of the area but also from the gaseous by-products of various industries.

In addition to industrial atmospheric pollution, the use of natural gas as a power source for heating the Westland glasshouse horticultural units, particularly in winter, results in sulphur dioxide contamination in this area. A careful check is kept on this sulphur dioxide content of the atmosphere by a network of continuously-recording meters in the south-western Randstad. Noticeable concentrations of atmospheric pollution are found here and it is clear that the refineries on the one hand and space heating on the other are the two major sources of pollution.

Nevertheless, the question of competition for land, or of land-use planning to reconcile the needs of housing, industry, services, transport, and recreation, is the major problem in the Randstad. Regional plans for municipalities, or groups of municipalities, are in existence for the entire area. The implementation of these plans, so that the essential character of the Randstad is not lost, depends on a careful balance between national planning (to encourage the development and growth of other areas in the Netherlands) and local planning to ensure the best use of the assets of this particular region. The future is certain to be a challenging one.

Further Work

A number of valuable sources for the geography of the Randstad are available in English studies of the Netherlands. These include:

BURKE, L. *The Making of Dutch Towns*, Cleaver Hume (1956)

BURKE, L. *Greenheart Metropolis*, Macmillan (1966)

HUGGETT, E. *The Modern Netherlands*, Pall Mall Press (1971)

LAMBERT, A. M. *The Making of the Dutch Landscape*, Seminar Press (1971).

The first two of these deal essentially with the urban scene, from a historical and a town-planning point of view respectively. They also give a reasonable amount of background detail and are well illustrated.

The third book is not illustrated (apart from one general map) and is a general study of the country from a historical, social, and political viewpoint. It provides a useful bibliography. Finally, Dr. Lambert's book is a mine of detailed information on the entire geography of the country, being completely up-to-date in its study and not historical as the title might imply. A comprehensive index and bibliography are also included in this well-illustrated book.

A general survey of the Randstad forms chapter 4 in:

HALL, P. *The World Cities*, World University Library (1966).

Details of reclamation and diking, etc. may be found in:

WAGRET, P. *Polderlands*, Methuen (1968).

Statistical data relating to the Netherlands is available in English in the *Statistical Yearbook of the Netherlands*, available from the Government Printing Office, The Hague. Many other statistical data are also published with an English list of contents at least but, unfortunately, a further useful source of information is only available in Dutch. This is the statistical handbook *Statistisch Zakboek* also published annually. A useful atlas, containing up-to-date maps of the Netherlands is *De Grote Bosatlas*, published by Wolters-Noordhoff, Groningen. In English, a further invaluable atlas to studies of Western Europe is of course the *Oxford Regional Economic Atlas of Western Europe*, O.U.P. (1971) which contains a general map of the Randstad area.

Other official Dutch government publications (available from the Government Printing Office in The Hague) have been prepared in English on aspects of planning and policy in the Netherlands. Amongst these are the following, all inexpensive and well illustrated: *Agriculture in the Netherlands* (1968); *The Delta Project* (1971); *Structure Plan for the Southern IJsselmeerpolders*, Rijkswaterstaat Communications, number 6, (1964).

Articles and maps in the *Tijdschrift voor Economische en Sociale Geografie*, published by the Royal Dutch Geographical Society (Koninklijk Nederlands Aardrijkskundig Genootschap) are frequently on topics concerned with the Netherlands and, where not in English, have a summary in that language. Chapter 7 in this book takes account of the following articles: J. Buursink, 'De Nederlandse hiërarchie der regionale centra', *T.E.S.G.* 1971, *62*, pp. 67–81; H. J. Keuning, 'A provisional concept of a functional division of the Netherlands', *T.E.S.G.* 1964, *55*, pp. 141–2; W. Steigenga, 'Recent planning problems of the Netherlands' in *Regional Studies*, 1968, *2*, pp. 105–18; D. Hazelhoff, 'Physical urbanisation of the Netherlands', *T.E.S.G.*, 1964, *55*, pp. 202–4.

The official mapping organization for the Netherlands has its main sales office at Delft. A comprehensive coverage of the whole country includes coloured topographic maps at 1:25 000 and 1:50 000 scales and smaller. Additionally, the three main municipalities (Amsterdam, The Hague, and Rotterdam) also maintain mapping organizations producing large-scale topographic and thematic maps.

Finally, and of considerable significance, the existence should be noted of the Information and Documentation Centre for the Geography of the Netherlands at the Rijksuniversiteit, Geografisch Instituut, Heidelberglaan, Utrecht, 2. This acts as a clearing house for publications on the Netherlands and publishes material collating data relating to the geography of the country as a whole.

Appendix

Population of the urban municipalities of the Randstad at 1 January 1971.

		Population 1.1.71	Density persons/sq. km			Population 1.1.71	Density persons/sq. km
*49	Alblasserdam S.H.†	18 104	2 074	25	Laren N.H.	14 179	1 145
67	Amersfoort U.	78 908	3 007	33	Leiden S.H.	100 135	4 464
19	Amstelveen N.H.	70 202	1 742	32	Leiderdorp S.H.	15 346	1 325
18	Amsterdam N.H.	820 406	4 823	38	Leidschendam S.H.	29 890	850
9	Assendelft N.H.	8 117	265	59	Maarssen U.	14 797	526
65	Baarn U.	24 315	740	63	Maartensdijk U.	8 574	216
17	Bennebroek N.H.	5 388	3 097	41	Maasluis S.H.	27 369	3 664
11	Beverwijk N.H.	41 029	2 215	22	Naarden N.H.	17 268	862
64	Bilt, de U.	29 514	1 032	48	Nieuwlekkerland	6 515	634
24	Blaricum N.H.	6 342	622	45	Nieuwerkerk a/d Ijssel S.H.	10 274	569
13	Bloemendaal N.H.	19 163	505	31	Oegstgeest S.H.	16 553	2 225
26	Bussum N.H.	41 372	5 095	20	Ouder-Amstel N.H.	8 445	335
40	Delft S.H.	86 189	3 319	53	Papendrecht S.H.	18 311	2 076
21	Diemen N.H.	10 491	931	50	Ridderkerk S.H.	43 552	1 830
70	Doorn U.	9 926	448	44	Rotterdam S.H.	679 032	4 111
54	Dordecht S.H. (with 55)	100 935	1 403	29	Rijnsburg S.H.	8 846	1 499
69	Driebergen-Rijsenburg U.	15 945	607	39	Rijswijk S.H.	50 482	2 806
58	Gorinchem S.H.	26 972	2 624	43	Schiedam S.H.	83 313	4 563
36	's-Gravenhage S.H. (The Hague)	537 643	8 232	56	Sliedrecht S.H.	20 202	1 586
				66	Soest U.	37 469	815
15	Haarlem N.H.	172 612	5 748	60	Utrecht U.	278 417	5 445
57	Hardinxveld-Giessendam S.H.	14 120	846	30	Valkenburg S.H.	2 853	522
10	Heemskerk N.H.	29 354	1 083	12	Velsen N.H.	67 501	1 542
16	Heemstede N.H.	26 386	2 884	42	Vlaardingen S.H.	81 097	3 376
51	Hendrik-Ido-Ambacht S.H.	14 250	1 337	37	Voorburg S.H.	44 207	7 028
				34	Voorschoten S.H.	21 765	1 956
27	Hilversum N.H.	98 948	2 164	62	Vreeswijk U.	5 572	756
23	Huizen N.H.	21 843	1 397	35	Wassenaar S.H.	27 623	542
1	Jisp N.H.	1 023	121	8	Westzaan N.H.	4 453	464
61	Jutphaas U.	7 166	299	2	Wormer N.H.	10 167	766
28	Katwijk S.H.	36 914	2 706	3	Wormerveer N.H.	14 760	2 923
6	Koog a/d Zaan N.H.	5 934	2 355	7	Zaandam N.H.	65 981	3 513
47	Krimpen a/d Lek S.H.	5 335	835	5	Zaandijk N.H.	6 052	3 713
46	Krimpen a/d Ijssel S.H.	19 316	2 698	14	Zandvoort N.H.	15 700	493
4	Krommenie N.H.	14 480	3 148	68	Zeist U.	56 187	1 127
				52	Zwijndrecht S.H.	32 412	2 212

The total population of these 70 municipalities amounts to 4 353 104

*These figures refer to the numbering on Fig. 1.
†N.H.: North Holland province; S.H.: South Holland province; U: Utrecht.

Index

Aalsmeer 13, 18
administrative organization 42, 43
agriculture 18–21; arable 20; cattle and livestock 21; size of holdings 21
air freight 37
airports 37
air traffic 37
Amersfoort 12
Amsterdam agglomeration 10, 29; industries and trade 11, 23; residential areas 10, 11
Amsterdam–Rhine Canal 35

Berkel 13
boezem 16
Bollenstreek 12, 18
Boskoop 13, 20
Burke, L. 8, 46
Buursink, J. 31

Caland Canal 33
Central Region 15, 16
container handling 38

Delft 13
Delta Plan 43
dike ii

European Economic Community 27, 32
Europoort 11, 13, 22, 23, 32, 38, 43

flower production 18

Gelderland 18
geographical themes 17, 39, 44
Gooi, Het 10, 11

Haarlem 11, 12
Haarlemmermeer polder 16
Hall, P. 10, 46
Hague, The 8, 9, 10, 13, 42
Hilversum 14
Holland ii
Hoogovens 22, 23, 38
Hook of Holland 13, 38
horticulture 18, 19

industries 22–4; iron and steel 22, 23; manufacturing 24; oil and chemicals 23; service 24
industrial problems 44, 45
information services 46
IJmond 10, 12
IJmuiden 22, 23

K.L.M. 37
Kennemerland, North 10, 12
Kennemerland, South 11, 12
Keuning, H. J. 31
Kring region 18

Lambert, A. M. 46
land use planning 45
Limburg 38
Limburg coalfield 22, 23, 39
Little Ring 28, 42

Maasvlakte 13, 22, 23
maps, official series 46; municipal 46
market gardening 18
motor vehicles 35
motorways 35
municipalities 30, 47; population figures 47

Netherlands, Statistical Yearbook of the 25, 27, 46
New Waterway 13, 18, 22, 23, 33, 38, 42
North Sea Canal 11, 22, 35
nuclear power station (Petten) 22

Physical Planning, Dutch Government Report on 8, 25, 39, 40, 42, 46
pipelines 11, 13, 37
planning 39–43
plassen 15, 16, 41
polders, reclamation stages 15, 16
pollution 44, 45
population 25–7; changes 29; characteristics 26, 27; density 25, 26; distribution 25, 26; growth rates 27
population growth 39, 44
population pattern (expected in A.D. 2000) 40
powerlines 38
projects, major 42

provinces, population 8
pumping 16

Randstad, central region 15; land heights in 11; major resource 8; municipalities 6, 48; name 8; physical limits 7, 8; size 8; sub-divisions 10
railways 14, 35; commuting patterns 36; future plans 43; urban metro lines 37, 43; intercity timings 36
refineries, oil 11, 13, 22, 23, 45
Rijnland coastal areas 12
Rijnsburg 12
roads 35
road developments
Rotterdam agglomeration 13; airport 32, 37; industries, trade 12, 23

Scheveningen 13
Schiphol 11, 32, 35, 37, 43
Southern IJsselmeer polders 37, 43
Structure Plan for A.D. 2000

Tijdschrift voor Economische en Sociale Geografie (*T.E.S.G.*) 31, 46
town growth 28
towns and urbanization 29–31
transport and communications 32–8; air traffic 37; freight 32; passenger 35; railways 35; roads 35; urban 37; water 32

urban agglomerations 30
urban development in Western Europe 42
urban hierarchies 30, 31
urban occupations 29
urbanization 28, 29
Utrecht 9, 14
Utrecht glacial ridge 14

Wassenaar 13
water control 44; zones 15
Westerland 13, 18, 42, 45

Zaan, the 12
Zaandvoort 12

Only the chief references to the main towns in the Randstad are indexed above; pictures and maps are included where the reference is significant.